#WDTFIMT??

A Gentle Rude Awakening to Become Selfless

By

EB

DEDICATIONS

I would like to thank God for EVERYTHING. If it weren't for Him pushing me to follow Him blindly with my eyes wide open, I wouldn't be writing this today.

R n R – You may not know what this book means to me now, but I know as you get older you will find a meaning for yourself. I know that you will always walk in purpose and wisdom – while being the AWESOME kids that you are. I love you.

The One – Life always seems to stand still when you come to my mind (every day)…And it is in those moments where I only want the best for you even if I am not part of your life. I still love you for who you are and who you are purposed to be. That will never change.

Pastor and First Lady – Thank you for being who you are. If there were more people like you, this world would definitely be a better place. Your love can NEVER be replicated. Your worth can NEVER be spent.

Dr. Mason – You know how to strike a nerve and I'm sure this is not the end of it. I look forward to more accountability moments, as I kick and scream throughout the process. Thank you for believing in me when I diminish myself.

Pops – Thank you for accepting me for who I am. You always say you're not normal, but as your "child" I have your traits as well and I am proud of it. You have always been a man of truth and I truly love you for that.

Nat – Our paths crossed when we were teenagers trying to conquer our own world. Now we are women destined for the whole world. Our journey will be one to impact the Joseph and Campbell supporters forever. ☺

Micki – Although things are what they are, as I write this, there is always that Faith Cliff to jump off of when we're ready. You were always one to challenge me to get over myself and to do what God has called me to do.

The #WDTFIMT Foreword

This is why I was born…
This is why I was placed on the earth…
All of my life has prepared me for **this** moment…

The immediate problem that I have with all of these statements is simply not being 100% confident that I know the answers. How can we know with certainty what God placed within us? How do we know that we are on the right path? How will our "inner self" agree with God that we finally get it? We start by believing a simple God fact: Over seven billion times God has created a person in HIS image, and he has not run out of distinct fingerprints yet! The care and love that is reserved for you by our Father begins with your purpose.

These pages do not have answers, rather within each entry of #WDTFIMT you will find prompts to dig deeper into the soil of your heart, nuggets to be discovered, seeds to be planted, and treasures to be unearthed. So please strap up, and prepare to scratch, claw, and do whatever is necessary to get God's best for your life. There is a sweet aroma, which lingers in your very being, after spending time in HIS presence. This book should be a part of the dedicated time that you spend with the Father. In addition to your devotion time, your prayer time, and your time to read God's Word. This is a time to actualize your destiny, clarify your purpose, and align all other parts of your life (career, family, service within your church, etc.) under this umbrella. Your very life will be changed as a result!

When we have come to the end of our earthly journey the question will remain: did he or she complete the assignments God gave to them? A true sense of accomplishment doesn't happen by completing random acts of service. Rather, true accomplishment is tethered to the act of yielding to God's designs for you that were written before the foundation of the world. So now comes the two hardest parts – Emptying yourself of anything that is contrary to God's plans for your life, and allowing God to fill your empty vessel and in so doing give it meaning and value.

The journey begins, anew, today! Take this book and read it, ingest it, accept it, apply it, and grow closer to God because of it! What a journey awaits you!

Dr. John L. Mason
Atlanta, Georgia

The #WDTFIMT Journey

If you are reading this book, I would first have to say "Thanks" for even thinking to pick it up to read it. Writing this book has most definitely been a kicking and screaming experience for me. There are a lot of things that I have been instructed to do, by God, when it comes to this book…and I have seriously looked in God's direction as if He was playing a joke on me. This is something that I NEVER saw myself doing, but it goes to show that our personal plans aren't always as concrete as we would like to believe they are.

Many people have asked me, "What in the world does #WDTFIMT mean???" It means "Where does this fit in my testimony?" I can admit, that each time I am asked that question, it is further confirmation that I'm on the right track to get people's attention. I've spent days at a time questioning if I am doing the right thing, would people even care, or would I be a person to impact other peoples' lives. I can't lie…I still have those questions, but as you read this book I pray that it touches you in such a way that you will never see yourself the same. I challenge you to take the next few months to let every word penetrate your spirits – so much that you would want to just escape to be in the presence of God to get away from yourself. Yes, I do have those moments and to even put those moments into words seems impossible.

There will never be an end to this Selfless Journey. It is something that is designed to become a part of your being, your make-up, and your way of life. You will not get it right from the very beginning. There will be times where you want to throw in the towel and give yourself a pink slip…but you have to remember this is not about you operating in your own strength. Here are some things to consider or have on hand as you embark on this journey:

- **Fast** – Pray about what or EVEN who you need to fast from. It will be revealed to you.

- **Bible** – Scriptures will be included in each passage, but I would really want you to study Word as it is given to you as well.

- **Journal** – Yes…I know this is already a "journal", but believe me when I say that there will be days that you need 8 packs of paper to write what is in your heart. Write down your prayers. List all people that you need to forgive and why (Including YOURSELF!). Write down the visions and plans that God gives you.

- **Accountability Partner** – In as much as I don't like people in my business, I know I still need to be accountable within this #WDTFIMT Journey. I suggest you choose someone that will not feel sorry for you when you want to have your own VIP Pity Party.

The Anatomy of #WDTFIMT

The coolest thing about this book is the fact that you do not have to read the book in the order it was printed. Truth be told, the way the book was printed is not the actual order it was written. How befitting right? Each #WDTFIMT entry is constructed as such:

- **The Opening** – Each opening may contain a fun fact, a general statement, or a thought provoking statement. Each opening is purposed to get you to prepare for everything else that your eyes will read and your conscience will awaken.

- **#WDTFIMT Moment** – I sometimes am convinced that God is sitting on His throne watching my life as if it is an Oscar-winning comedy. Each #WDTFIMT Moment is a self-reflection of an event, my personal feelings, or just everyday life.

- **#WDTFIYOURT Challenge** – What good would it do for you to read this book if you do not change for the better? Each #WDTFIYOURT (Where Does This Fit In Your Testimony) Challenge makes you look beyond your current situation in conjunction with the entry that you have read. I have to be honest. You may have some uncomfortable moments with yourself as you complete a "challenge", but I would say that being uncomfortable for a moment will be more than worth it for the long run.

- **The Questions** – You are asked the same questions after every entry.

  - **Where does this fit in your testimony?** – Whether if you have experienced the same situation or not, how can you relate to the entry?

- ○ **What is the take away?** – We cannot change everything in one day…But what is the one thing that you can reflect on in order to improve an area within your life?
- ○ **What are you thankful for?** – Despite what life throws at us, there is always something to be thankful for.
- ○ **Who can you do something nice for?** – Giving back is always a good thing. Whether if it is a small deed or big deed, there is someone that you can make smile…event if it is for a moment.

- **Study Notes** – You are not expected to be a bible scholar by the time you get done with this book…But studying the Word and applying the Word can never hurt.

I pray that you will see how AWESOME you are even during your worse moments. As you make it a point to get past self… Do the unthinkable, while achieving the impossible! You were created for this!

Madd ♥ EB

This book is not meant to be read in the order that it was printed. Pick a title that stands out to you. Let the journey begin!

Your Poop Stinks Too!

I sometimes wonder what God was thinking when He destined me to do what I do. And the reason why I say that is because He gives me revelations at the WEIRDEST times of the day and all I can do is follow-through with what He has given me. With that being said...This is one of those entries where I have to put a disclaimer out there. What type of disclaimer? I don't know...I guess for those that are embarrassed of bodily functions, you should be aware that this may make you blush. That's the best way that I can put it....

#WDTFIMT Moment

Yesterday I was in a public bathroom. As many of you may know, public bathrooms aren't the best and it makes you wonder if people treat their own bathrooms as they would treat a public one. Needless to say...when you have to go you just have to go.

Side note...Have you ever wondered why bathrooms are also called restrooms? I'm going to have to research that one some more.

I sometimes feel that public bathrooms are like Vegas. What happens in the bathroom should stay in the bathroom. BUT we all know that is not the case. While using the bathroom, I could tell someone a few stalls down was having a fight with her stomach. It was one of those moments where you actual felt bad because having one of those fights with your stomach is not a pretty thing to go through. What is produced from that fight is not pretty either...The sounds, the smell, etc. In the midst of this fight, you can hear people at the sink snickering and making comments as they washed their hands. Thus, making me feel bad even more for this person. I'm sure she was already humiliated by having this stomach fight in a public bathroom, but to be ridiculed for it makes it even worse. Whoever was at the sink obviously broadcasted it once they left the bathroom, because I could still hear the jokes and laughter outside as I began to wash my hands. And then it hit me...how can we make fun of the way someone's poop smells when ours stink too. It's no different than sin. We talk about what sin everyone else commits and judge them for their sin, but we fail to look at what we do.

You may be asking yourself was I truly in the bathroom analyzing this in my head? YES. It was as if I had no choice. It's as if these things are noticeable in a whole different dimension than what I would normally look at it as. Having bad personal habits of hygiene is one thing...Believe me, you can tell when you are using the bathroom right behind someone who lacks hygiene etiquette. But one can follow all of the best hygiene rules and just end up having a stomach fight in the bathroom. As I thought about this, I began to feel convicted about the times that I made fun of how someone else's poop smelled…And then I began to question who I have unrightfully judged for any sin that they may have committed. I thought of the times when I would hold my breath and make comments to myself or even to someone else…wishing that some people would just do a couple of courtesy flushes. BUT sometimes those courtesy flushes don't help either. Even if you are in a bathroom that had air fresheners…that doesn't always help. The smell and everything else is just exposed, while you have to find a way to deal with it especially if you really have to use the bathroom. No different than sin. When sin is exposed there are only but a few options on how to deal with it.

When we look at the sin in our life, who are we to judge anyone else for what they do? Sadly to say we sin by choice. Pooping just happens when the body is ready to do so. Yes, we can choose where we poop but in some instances, there is no time to wait. With sin, we choose what sin we commit. With sin, we choose how to commit the sin. With sin, we choose where to commit the sin. With sin, we choose who to commit the sin against or with. We may sin, but we then turn around and judge people for the same thing that we may have done 5 minutes ago.

Gossip
Lying STEALING
EXaggerating
Judging Others
Etc. Etc. Etc.

We all know that there is a LONG list of sins. How ironic is it that we can keep up with the list of someone else's sins…BUT we tend to forget that the list even exists when we commit a sin. I challenge you, today, to remember that as much as your poop stinks…Your sin reeks of an unpleasant smell as well. Next time you go to the bathroom and someone is having a stomach fight, just put yourself in their shoes and judge yourself.

#WDTFIYOURT Challenge

I don't know what your thoughts are at this moment. Do you feel the need to take a moment and think about how you may have judged others? Better yet, do you need to reflect on how it has made you feel when others have wrongfully judged you. What "smells" need to be freshened up in your life? Some things, from your perspective, may be hard to turn away from…But really, by keeping up with certain sins how far have you gotten in life. Begin to acknowledge each sin for what they are. Be transparent with yourself and ask yourself why you keep doing the same thing. As you strive to change your ways from the notable sins, turn to God on a daily basis and ask for Him to give you the strength to get past anything that is not of Him. While you're at it…forgive those that have sinned against you and encourage others around you to do the same. Start today by making a "Change List" and list ways that you can change.

#WDTFIMT Reading/Meditation

- ❑ Romans 2
- ❑ Matthew 7:1-5

Where does this fit in your testimony?

_____

_____

_____

_____

_____

Based on what you read, what is your main take away? And why?

_____

_____

_____

_____

_____

What are you thankful for today? Why?

_____

_____

_____

Who can you do something nice for today? And how?

_____

_____

_____

_____

_____

_____

Study Notes

_____
_____
_____
_____
_____
_____
_____
_____
_____
_____
_____
_____
_____
_____
_____
_____
_____
_____
_____
_____
_____
_____
_____
_____
_____
_____
_____
_____
_____
_____
_____
_____

There's A Hole in My Straw!!

Whoever came up with the idea of a drinking straw was pure genius. The invention of the drinking straw is dated back to 3000 BC but wasn't technically patented until 1888. Since then we were gifted with silly straws, bendy straws...even the reusable straws that comes with the thermal cups nowadays. It's an invention that makes you say "I wish I was the first one to come up with that Idea!"...But there is obviously a reason why none of us can say that.

#WDTFIMT Moment

Have you ever had one of your favorite drinks in front of you and the moment you took a sip from the straw that drink didn't make it into your mouth...Only because there was a hole in the straw? That has happened plenty of times and it is quite frustrating, to be honest. One day I had my favorite Mango Tango drink in my possession. I put it in the freezer to give it a little slush. Then I added some Greens (a product of It Works) to it and I was ready to enjoy one of the best drinks in the world. Apparently, the straw that was in my bottle had a different agenda. It was as if the straw woke up that day telling itself it would give me a hard time for whatever reason. I took a sip through the straw...only bits and pieces of my slush drink came through. I thought there was something lodged in the middle. I took the straw out, blew into it really hard and tried again. Still the same result when I took my next sip. The drink that my body craved was being re-filtered back into the bottle - not making it anywhere into my mouth.

Of course in any of my weird life moments, I think of things from a different point of view. While I threw a fit about me not being able to enjoy my drink, I started to think about how our spirits crave certain things from God...BUT because we have holes somewhere in our lives we can't get the full source of whatever it is that we seek from Him. Every time we try to take a sip of what we can get from God, there is a disconnect from the source to our spirits. Our expectations drives us to blame the "straw". We continuously take sips only to end up with nothing but air...as we hear that annoying sound that a straw makes whenever it has a hole in it.

#WDTFIYOURT Challenge

I don't know what holes are stopping your source flow, but now is the time to re-examine some things and believe that those holes will no longer exist – allowing you to benefit from the source that you seek. You can have holes in your heart, mind, finances, family, etc. Whatever it is, you can only sip through that holey straw but for so long. Make it a point today to determine if you need to just get a new straw. God wants us to have access to all sources that He intended for us to have as we fulfill our purpose in life. Write down all areas of your life where holes exist. Have you contributed to the hole or have you allowed others to help for the hole? List ways on how you can make sure that holes are no longer a factor in whatever area of your life. Based on that list, put in place an action plan on how to move forward. You will not be able to accomplish everything in one day, but the only thing that matters (at this point) is that you start to make a change.

#WDTFIMT Reading/Meditation

- ❑ Ephesians 4:17-24
- ❑ Romans 8:18-39

Where does this fit in your testimony?

Based on what you read, what is your main take away? And why?

What are you thankful for today? Why?

Who can you do something nice for today? And how?

Study Notes

Matters of the Heart That Are Tied to the Mind

I don't think there is a "formal" introduction to this one. There are a lot of issues that we face today that we can call "Matters of The Heart"...But would you agree that those matters are always tied to the mind?

#WDTFIMT Moment

There is a particular issue that I'm dealing with. One that I wouldn't wish on anyone because it just seems too puzzling. Somewhat irritating, confusing, and everything else that I can't describe right now. If I could hit the fast forward button to bypass all of the feelings and roller coasters of emotions...I would. I think I've kept myself busy and distracted to not have to process anything from this issue...but somehow my mind always catches up to it.

When you look at the matters of the heart, somehow your mind starts to run a mile a minute with doubt, questions, etc. It eventually gets to a point where your mind runs so far that you start doubting and questioning yourself. You start asking yourself "What is wrong with me?"..."Am I not good enough?"..."What did I do wrong?" Let it (your mind) run even further and you can come up with everything that is wrong with you, why you're not good enough and what you did wrong. The mind is a terrible thing to waste...But it is also something that you wouldn't want to let loose. If that makes sense.

In all of this, I can only trust in a strength that is stronger than my natural ability. There have been days of tears. There have been days of me feeling that I should give up and walk away from everything...But there is always that ounce of hope that things will get better and I wouldn't have invested myself, heart, and all for nothing. It is that small still, but powerful voice that is telling me that I did nothing wrong, I am good enough, and that there isn't anything wrong with me.

The "Matters of The Heart" are measured differently from person to person. It may be relationship issues for one, while for another it may be a financial issue. Whatever it may be for you, untie your mind from that matter to hear that still, but powerful, voice.

#WDTFIYOURT Challenge

Take a moment to list in your journal anything/everything that is aching your heart. After that, write down what your thoughts are in regards to each situation/matter. Do you dare ask yourself if you are allowing each situation/matter to take over you in such a way that you are reasoning yourself to death? Take the rest of the day and ask God what needs to be done in regards to each situation/matter. Do you need to completely let go of whatever it may be and allow God to take over?

#WDTFIMT Reading/Meditation

- ❑ Psalm 7
- ❑ Romans 12:14-23

Where does this fit in your testimony?

_____

_____

_____

_____

_____

Based on what you read, what is your main take away? And why?

_____

_____

_____

_____

_____

What are you thankful for today? Why?

_____

_____

_____

Who can you do something nice for today? And how?

_____

_____

_____

_____

_____

_____

Study Notes

Matters of the Warped Mind

Depression....Enough said.

#WDTFIMT Moment

Has anyone ever lived on this earth and not go through some form of depression? I can't answer that question factually, but I would take an educated guess and say no. Depression is a "no-no" word. In today's society, we are not encouraged to express how we honestly feel (specifically mentally and emotionally) let alone express concerns of self-depression.

I'm sure there are different forms of depression. In those various forms, we live our everyday lives as if things are normal...But things are not normal. One that is depressed may spend days in darkness (physically/emotionally/mentally) while doing his/her best to avoid as much human contact as possible. One that is depressed is a prisoner within his/her own mind. One that is depressed may feel that no one will understand, but the reality is EVERYONE would understand.

In my days of trying to figure things out (based on a recent event in life), I can only see the beauty in this darkness. As twisted as that may sound, these past few days have not been the best let alone attractive. I've seen life in a whole different way, while not trying to convince myself that I am the problem. I've replayed the situation in my mind until I became paralyzed with the continuous thoughts of why did I even allow myself to think things would be different this time. I've disappeared from life the best way that I know how...But I'm still breathing. And that is the beauty in this.

Some may judge me for being in the state that I'm in, but I can only be honest where I am. Taking away the title of me being a mother. Taking away the title of whatever title that has been given to me voluntarily and involuntarily...At the end of the day, my mind has held itself captive and I would be lucky if I can decipher what is important at the moment. If you were to ask me what is important and not ask my mind, I would tell you that being able to sleep in peace is what is important right now...But my mind has other plans.

#WDTFIYOURT Challenge

Think about what you are dealing with today that has your mind all over the place. Are you on the brink of retreating away from the world? Are you ashamed to admit the feelings that you are having? Are you ashamed to reveal the thoughts that you are thinking? PLEASE know that you are not alone in your current state. Reach out to someone that you trust. If you can't trust anyone, then really find someone that is a professional that would just listen to you. I would be bold to say call me if you run out of options. 478.5MyPath. I may not be able to solve world hunger, but I have an ear that will listen to your heart.

#WDTFIMT Reading/Meditation

- ❑ Romans 12:1-8
- ❑ Psalm 139

Where does this fit in your testimony?

_____

_____

_____

_____

_____

Based on what you read, what is your main take away? And why?

_____

_____

_____

_____

_____

What are you thankful for today? Why?

_____

_____

_____

Who can you do something nice for today? And how?

_____

_____

_____

_____

_____

_____

Study Notes

Matters of a Broken Heart

Question…Does anyone know why most country singers sound so heartbroken? For the life of me, I have always tried to understand the reasons why and could never wrap my head around it. One thing that I can relate to these country singers with is the whole broken heart.

#WDTFIMT Moment

I love hard…I just don't love anyone. Yes, I love people even when my feelings don't want to…But I'm talking about the love that would make you give your life for someone else without a second thought. With that love, you get the unseen bargain. There is a bargain that promises a happily ever after. And there's the other bargain that you pray doesn't happen because if it does…the world (as you have known it to be with love) will forever be different.

Due to recent events that have transpired, I think I am retired from love. The aftermath of a broken heart is so indescribable – at least with written words. If you were to ask me to put some type of reference to it, I would say that it feels as if someone has stopped the airflow to your lungs and you still try to function as if nothing has happened. At some point, life begins to have less meaning because the broken heart can't enjoy life. It can't do anything but try to find at least an ounce of blood to reach its arteries to make it feel normal again.

What do you do when you've loved beyond expectations and promises were made only to be broken? What do you do when your heart becomes molded for one person only…only to have to forcefully reshape that mold when things come to an end? I'm sure you've gotten the picture on where I am with this. I would be the first to say that there is nothing healthy about having a broken heart. Mentally you begin to beat yourself up as if you were the total blame. Emotionally…you'd rather rub onions on your eyes than to feel the emotional pain. Physically, you lose yourself in weight gain and weight loss – ultimately feeling unattractive in the long-run. Spiritually, you question God before you question if you heard God the first time about the broken relations.

To be honest, I do know if I have words of encouragement within this. But for the sake of us growing, as we embark on this journey together, let me dig deep.

#WDTFIYOURT Challenge

Only God knew that you would be where you are in life today. He knew what was going to happen. Who was going to be a part of what happens. And the overall outcome of how you handle what happened. Have you considered that God may have wanted you to see something differently in the situation other than your broken heart? Meditate not only on the lesson but practice your testimony. Someone else will need to hear it.

#WDTFIMT Reading/Meditation

- ❑ Isaiah 41
- ❑ Psalm 34

Where does this fit in your testimony?

_____

_____

_____

_____

_____

Based on what you read, what is your main take away? And why?

_____

_____

_____

_____

_____

What are you thankful for today? Why?

_____

_____

_____

Who can you do something nice for today? And how?

_____

_____

_____

_____

_____

_____

Study Notes

Do You Really Know What Love Is?

Does anyone really know how or why Valentine's Day originated? If you were to Google its meaning you, will receive over a million results in less than 0.012 seconds. As February 14 approaches, millions of dollars would be spent by people that feel obligated to do something for someone that they may not truly love...BUT for the sake of keeping peace, they comply with the V-Day hype to only go back to everyday life on February 15.

#WDTFIMT Moment

When it comes to holidays, I may only wink at the thought of becoming stressed out about following every rule for whatever holiday that is to be celebrated. Valentine's Day is no exception. Why just choose one day out of the year to shower a person that you "love" with gifts and a night out? Seriously??? Is that person's worth only valuable enough for you to comply with a holiday one day out of the year to show your "love" for them?

Love is something that is not to be taken lightly and there is proof that many do take it lightly. People pick and choose moments of love when it's convenient for them, but then they throw a fit when another person treats them the same way. People give 30 percent of themselves, but expect others to give 1,000 percent back. What would this world be like if everyone gave their all when it comes to love 365 days of the year - every minute that they are living and breathing??

It's been a true test of my Love Walk these past few months. There are so many examples that I can give, but I don't think we have time for that. Each situation always leads back to the same thing...Am I willing to love as I have been commanded to? God has been pushing me to love so much in one situation...I honestly don't know how much more I can give. I don't know if I can keep going even at times when it hurts or seems unbearable. You may say love isn't supposed to hurt and I would disagree. Love only hurts when you are willing to let go of your former ways...when you let go of selfish ways in the name of love. There is nothing peaceful about that as you go through the process. Just as long as you go through that process. I don't know how much more of myself I can reveal through the walls that were broken down...And I just have to be real with you on that. I'm walking and giving my love in the most impossible situation, but I can only trust God. I've done it before...But oddly this situation trumps all situations and it's just one of those things that you ask yourself do you really have it in you or are you just done with it all? I'm walking and giving my love even when I just want to throw in the towel - telling God that I've done all that I can. I'm walking and giving my love when it is the most uncomfortable feeling to ever feel - asking God would any of this mean a hill of beans in the long run. I'm walking and giving my love when I can just walk away and not think twice about it. I'm walking and giving my love when every thought within my mind rages a war between right from wrong. And even in all of this...all I can do is love. I have to love even when things are silent. I have to love even when things seem impossible. I have to love 100 percent because God doesn't give me any less.

Love shouldn't be forced. Love is not out of convenience. Love is not based on feelings. Love is not to give only to receive something in return. Love doesn't hold on to wrong doings. Love is letting go of self to edify someone else even when they don't deserve it. Love is to love someone even when it is the most uncomfortable feeling. Love is loving someone so much that you love and care for their soul before you even love them. Love is the character of a mature person that truly knows what it means to love. Love is something that is given regardless of one's past or flaws. Love is why we wake up every day to walk in our true purpose and not just play the game of life.

#WDTFIYOURT Challenge

Do you really mean it when you tell someone you love them? Does it only show in your words or does it also show in your actions? Think of the things that have held you back from experiencing true love. It can be a lot of reasons. Once you've written everything down, make it a point to pray about each thing. What do you need to do to get past self in each area? It may be that you are holding onto unforgiveness. It may be that you've grown up not having any true examples of love in your life. I don't know what the reasons may be, but I challenge you to not allow any reason to remain an excuse in your life from this point forward. There is only one great example of love...and that example is God sending Jesus to this earth to die for our sins. Reflect on the life of Jesus and let Him be your true love example.

#WDTFIMT Reading/Meditation

- ❑ 1 Corinthians 13

Where does this fit in your testimony?

_____

_____

_____

_____

Based on what you read, what is your main take away? And why?

_____

_____

_____

_____

_____

What are you thankful for today? Why?

_____

_____

_____

Who can you do something nice for today? And how?

_____

_____

_____

_____

_____

Study Notes

Pray With Pain

It is one thing to have faith...But it's another thing to have your foundation of faith shaken in such a way that it'll make you buckle over, screaming within your soul to only feel as if you're breathing your last breath. Only then you'll know that you can only continue to stand within that faith and know that things are being worked out. - EB

#WDTFIMT Moment

Honestly...Today has been a day where I had to walk around with a smile on my face, while deep down inside I just wanted to buckle over and scream with frustration and pain. When I heard "Pray with Pain" a couple of days ago...I literally asked how I can put that into words. I had an idea, but truly at that moment, I was at a standstill on what to write...Until now.

The Bible states to count "it" (everything that you go through, experience, etc.) all joy. Sometimes I have to ask God if He was serious by having that verse in there. I'm sure some other people have asked the same thing as well. I think, today, I did more than ask if He was serious. I just let go of everything that I had inside of me. The pain and frustration were more intense than any natural disaster that this world may have ever seen...That's the best way that I can describe it. Now I can say I know what David felt when he experienced his moments of crying out to God. It's a cry that you let out feeling as if God doesn't hear you, but you push your way through to make sure He knows how you feel. Ironically, He knows what you feel before you even feel it, but honestly, in those moments, you tend to put that fact to the side because the pain you feel is indescribable.

It's a prayer of pain. It's a prayer that is filled with tears, words of frustration, and elevated voice tones. It's a prayer that puts you in a place where it's just you and God - nothing else matters at that moment. It's a prayer where you declare that if it takes everything out of you to get your words out then so be it...just as long as God hears you. It's a prayer that would make you feel inadequate, insecure, and everything else because you don't truly feel that God would even say something back once you got done. BUT you keep pushing forward because as you press through that pain you somehow know that you must have at least a mustard seed of faith regardless of how you may feel.

I don't know who is going through their "Prayer of Pain" moment or has already experienced it. All I can say is be honest with yourself and God as you go through it. As you go through the process, try to find a way to press through and stand on the foundation of faith that has brought you this far. It's not easy and it's not going to feel as if you're stopping to smell the roses. I would be one to know.

#WDTFIYOURT Challenge

Just take a few moments to let all pain go. Better yet…Take ALL day to let go of the pain. Whether if you have to cry until snot comes out your nose. Whether if you have to just talk to God until you get everything off of your chest…Do it! If you are prompted/moved to write in your journal, write whatever is in your heart.

#WDTFIMT Reading/Meditation

- ❑ Psalm 5
- ❑ Mark 11:20-26

Where does this fit in your testimony?

_____

_____

_____

_____

_____

Based on what you read, what is your main take away? And why?

_____

_____

_____

_____

_____

What are you thankful for today? Why?

_____

_____

_____

Who can you do something nice for today? And how?

_____

_____

_____

_____

_____

_____

_____

Study Notes

You're Fat...Lose Weight

Obesity...That is apparently the Nation's new epidemic - while other countries frown upon our citizens for being so "fat". Nowadays all you see are quick remedies of weight loss pills, cleansing juices, etc. According to statistics, there are more people that have gym memberships than there are people working out in the gym. It is one's best interest to be healthy and fit, but is that enough? We watch shows like "Nip Tuck" (seeing how much fat can be sucked out of a person's belly), but what about the fat in our spiritual lives. Fat consists of toxins that bring on other "issues". Have you seen what fat looks like? I'm not talking about the fat from cleaning chicken. I'm talking about the fat that can weigh someone down so much that they can't even move.

#WDTFIMT Moment

Before I have this moment, I need to make a disclaimer. Everyone's body image appears to be what it is for whatever reason. By no means am I ridiculing anyone's image based on their body size.

Now that we have that out of the way...

Weight loss pills...Done that. Juicing...Done that. I've tried a couple exercise machines...BUT those were returned. I've found something that I absolutely love, though!!! Zumba at Glitter's Fitness Club. When I say I'm addicted...I'm addicted. Don't get me wrong. I'm not one of those chicks that "hates" my body, but I had to be honest with myself on putting on a few pounds for not remaining healthy and active as I have done so before.

I was waiting on the train, the other day, and I saw a woman walk by. It was obvious that she was struggling with her weight. There are just some things that you can sense from people without them even saying anything. In that moment of seeing her, I felt sadness. I didn't know her story, but I absolutely couldn't assume her story either. People become overweight for a lot of reasons (i.e. Medical, Emotional, etc.). Either way, I couldn't try to figure out her reasons...It is what hit me at that moment that was something to pay attention to. I heard "Lose Weight"...And it didn't take long for me to figure out what weight needed to be lost.

People often assume that being physically overweight is the source of a lot of issues. What they don't factor in are the effects of those that are overweight spiritually, emotionally, and mentally. They don't understand that the core of one's body is not in the abdominal area, but the core of one's body and being is in the heart as well as the mind. You can't focus on one without the other. Take a moment to think about how your heart and mind are being weighed down. What "fat" do you need to lose? Once you begin the weight loss process it's never easy. Things get tensed. You feel things that you don't want to feel or have never felt before. You end up working against a resistance that can defeat you at any moment. BUT do you stop when you feel as if you can't go any longer? It's tempting. Believe me...I'd be the first to say that it is. I'd also be the first to say that there have been times where I've almost checked out of the Spiritually Fat Camp earlier than I needed to. But when you look at the bigger picture, your purpose is bigger than your fat. You'd have to lose your fat in order to fulfill your purpose.

#WDTFIYOURT Challenge

I don't know who's reading this today, but re-evaluate the fat in your life that is causing you to be overweight spiritually, emotionally, and mentally. What "exercises" do you need to put into your routine to help lose that weight? What "food" do you need to eat in order for you to have a healthier regimen in what you feed your heart and your mind? Only you know what you need to do. Only you know what you've been doing and haven't been doing. Don't make this weight loss another New Year's resolution. Make it your daily routine for the rest of your life as you walk within your purpose.

#WDTFIMT Reading/Meditation

- ❑ Ephesians 2:11-22
- ❑ Matthew 11:25-30

Where does this fit in your testimony?

_____

_____

_____

_____

_____

_____

Based on what you read, what is your main take away? And why?

_____

_____

_____

_____

_____

What are you thankful for today? Why?

_____

_____

_____

_____

Who can you do something nice for today? And how?

_____

_____

_____

_____

_____

_____

_____

_____

Study Notes

Be Naked With Trust

Adam and Eve knew to be "ashamed" of their nakedness once they encountered the enemy. People always debate whose fault it was for what took place that day, but nonetheless, we are at fault this present day for the things we allow ourselves to be "ashamed" of once we have our own personal encounters with the enemy. We put up walls so thick, that it's hard for us to see that God already placed the last period in our book of life - where we ultimately have the victory.

#WDTFIMT Moment

I apologize but I have to cut to the chase on this one. I couldn't find a more "softer" way to paint the picture for this topic. A few years back this revelation came to me..."Just as the trees are willing to be naked during the coldest seasons of their life...We are to be just as more willing to be naked before God. Trusting that even in those moments, He will still keep us alive and restore us." When it first came to me, of course, I went through my 21 questions series with God...But it is so true in everything that we deal with so what is there to question? I'm going to break down what that meant for me and hopefully....HOPEFULLY, you'll be able to see what it means for you, personally.

1. Trees lose their leaves like clockwork. We all know that once a tree's leaves change color, dry up, and fall to the ground the season is about to change. Something is about to happen. BUT trees willingly let their leaves fall. Even in the summer when it gets too hot and there hasn't been any rain, trees lose their leaves. I've never seen a tree put up a fight to keep its leaves. Why can't we be the same way in our coldest/hottest moments of life when we are being tested? Granted, we may not always know the signs before we encounter something, but I do know that most of us put up a fight to not lose our "leaves" when that storm/situation hits us. I struggle with that sometimes because in my mind I'm not supposed to be soft. I have to keep my game face on at all times...But to be real with you that fight becomes tiresome.

2. Trees lose their leaves knowing that they will grow back. I wouldn't be the one to say that a tree actually/literally knows that its leaves will grow back...BUT we as people know that if God made a way before then He is bound to do it again. That is of course if we're doing what we need to do within Him as well. There comes a point during that situation where God feeds us and rains on us enough for us to get our strength back to restore/enhance our "leaves" in a spiritual sense. So why do we put up a fight knowing that we'd come out of our storm/situation better than we started??

3. As the tree loses its leaves, it somehow goes through a resting period or cleansing process. We have to learn to be as a tree and rest within God while we are being cleansed for His purpose. Life throws so much at us on a regular basis and there is only but so much we can take. You may not be able to literally rest (a.k.a. sleep) during a storm/situation, but you can for surely rest within God (spiritually) knowing that He is in the storm/situation with you.

If you really look at it, we should never cover up ourselves in such a way that God cannot have access to us 100%. We have to get out of that frame of mind and know that in all things we are to be naked before God as we trust in His word and His promises. What good would our lives be without doing so?

#WDTFIYOURT Challenge

I don't know what any of you may be dealing with...BUT I do know that you can only be naked with trust in order to see the AWESOMENESS that God has in life for you. I've had to lose my "leaves", my mind, and even my own will a few weeks back in order to be able to blindly trust God with every storm/situation that is in my life. And as I say that, I even had to look at some things that I've allowed the enemy to make me feel ashamed for doing so. Give the enemy a one-way ticket to the Bermuda Triangle and send the feeling of being ashamed with him. Once you do that, make it a point to lose your "leaves" and trust that God would be able to restore or give you everything that you may feel that you've lost...A Hundred Fold.

#WDTFIMT Reading/Meditation

- ❑ Proverbs 3
- ❑ Luke 12:22-34

Where does this fit in your testimony?

_____

_____

_____

_____

_____

_____

Based on what you read, what is your main take away? And why?

_____

_____

_____

_____

_____

_____

What are you thankful for today? Why?

_____

_____

_____

_____

Who can you do something nice for today? And how?

_____

_____

_____

_____

_____

_____

_____

Study Notes

Life's Detours

I'm sure many of us have specific routes that we travel on a regular basis. Whether if it is by car, walking, or train, there is a route that we can practically follow with our eyes closed. Our routes become familiar as we trust those routes to lead us to our determined destination without any major issues. BUT there comes a point in time when we get ready to travel those routes and we somehow find a detour sign hindering us. Detours become a nuisance especially when we've planned our timing according to our normal routes. We are then put in the position to figure out how to maneuver this new detour and still get to our destination as planned.

#WDTFIMT Moment

I love the area that I live in simply for the fact that if I don't want to drive to work I can take the train. It's a simple 2-minute drive from the house and I can just park my car, while the train conductor can handle the rest. I also love where I live because it's a hop, skip, and a jump to get on the highway if I decide to drive. Well...My 2-minute drive has now become close to 5 minutes...While my hop, skip, and a jump has turned into a long walk. The bridge right in front of the train station is inoperable...sooooo that blocks me in 2 directions of anywhere I need to go and I have no choice but to follow this detour. It's frustrating because my destinations are so close, but this detour is in my way.

On my way, last night, to my newly found place to escape (Glitter's Fitness Club for Zumba) I got a "revelation" once I saw that annoying detour sign. If you realize, detours sometimes come up when you are so close to where you're heading. You're right there at the .04 mile mark and now you have to go another 3 miles because of a detour. And then you ask yourself "What sense does that make??!!!" Detours are a way of you not relying on self, but totally relying on God. Not only that, detours may be necessary for a reason that neither one of us would know but as we follow that detour we may find more of what we've been seeking within God, our prayer life, and life in general. I have at least 3 detours active in my life right now. For example, I've been in transition to decide what church to go to. I found one that I absolutely love without a doubt, but yet it's been set within me to visit another church this weekend. Although I haven't committed to the church that I absolutely love...I feel like I'm cheating on the newly loved church. But I have to accept the detour for what it is and only trust God to direct me. I have to accept all of the active detours in my life right now. Although we have choices in life, I know I might as well face the detours now because it's obvious that I need to see something within each and every one of them.

A lot of you may be experiencing some type of detour in life. As uncomfortable as it may be (Believe me...I have my moments of kicking and screaming) we have to come to a place of expecting something great to come out of the detours that we face. We may not be able to see that once we approach a detour sign...But something great is bound to happen as we follow the new course that we are being led on.

#WDTFIYOURT Challenge

What detours do you find yourself challenged with today? Better yet, ask yourself if you were initially traveling down a path that God never purposed to begin with and you are currently on a detour from your own plans. If you do not know the plan that God has for you, take the rest of the day...NO! Take as long as it is needed to seek God on the plan that He has for your life. As He reveals everything to you, write it down, and live it out.

#WDTFIMT Reading/Meditation

- ❏ Isaiah 45
- ❏ Deuteronomy 2:26-37

Where does this fit in your testimony?

_____

_____

_____

_____

_____

_____

Based on what you read, what is your main take away? And why?

_____

_____

_____

_____

_____

_____

What are you thankful for today? Why?

_____

_____

_____

_____

Who can you do something nice for today? And how?

_____

_____

_____

_____

_____

_____

_____

Study Notes

Promises and Broken Words

How many pinky promises did you make as a kid? I know I've made many and as I grew older the pinky promises were replaced with verbal promises. A lot of people fail to realize that they do not literally have to say "I Promise" to commit themselves to something. When we commit ourselves to something, we are actually making a promise. Some people do not realize that being true to who they are is also a way of keeping a promise. If they say they are loyal to something or someone...That's a promise. If they tell someone that they would be there for them no matter what...That's a promise. Promises are to be kept regardless of how one feels, is being treated, etc. Sadly to say, most promises are followed by broken words. Broken words come into play when a promise isn't fulfilled. Broken words come into play when one makes excuses for not wanting to make good on what they've committed to. Broken words ultimately lead to someone getting hurt, being disappointed, etc. The only exception to the "Promise Rule" would be if someone is being abused in some kind of way. I'd be the first to say that they can get a pass and not have to carry out their commitments but find a way to walk in love/forgiveness in order to be able to move on in life.

#WDTFIMT Moment

Many who know me knows not to commit to something if you're going to make an excuse to not follow through. I'm like that within my personal life and also when it comes to business (Also with how people handle their own businesses...That's a whole different topic). If you were to ask me if I'm more lenient in one area than I am in the other...I don't think I am. I'm one to say practice what you preach when dealing with me because if not I'd rather not deal with you at all. Honestly, that is something that I've been told to work on because not everyone may not be where I am today or at any given moment. Granted, I always take into consideration that things may come up BUT when it starts to be an excuse after excuse...I don't have the tolerance for it. I'm one to let you know if there would be a delay in me coming through with something, but when it's all said and done I make it a point to come through.

One thing that I have learned is that some "promises" are delayed and I'm still getting used to the fact that some "promises" are meant to be delayed. There are a lot of things that I've seen and known that is "promised". It is just a matter of waiting on those "promises" to come through, while I fulfill any promises that I've made regardless of how I feel, how someone acts, etc. In one particular situation that I'm facing now...I've had PLENTY of conversations with the devil. (Sidenote: If you don't know what it means to have a convo with the devil...Prepare yourself for when that time comes). From whispers of "You might as well give up!" and "You're trusting God for the impossible!" To actual heated moments of me professing and proclaiming the promises that I've made, have been made to me and all promises that I know of...It's literally a Nuclear War Zone at times. If I were to tell people certain things about this situation they'd say the same thing the devil has said and I don't have time for that. There comes a time in life where you have to look plum crazy in the eyes of the Devil and other people when standing on the promises of God. And the funny thing is...I'm looking even crazier for standing on the promises that I know God gave to someone else. That's where that promise of "I'll be there for you no matter what" comes into play. Whoever you made that commitment to may be going through hell, but because of that promise, you're willing to go through hell with them because you may be the stronger one at that point. And as I'm walking and typing at the same time...that revelation just came to me and it has answered main questions that I've been asking..."What's the point...Why me and why now?" Ultimately it all goes back to purpose and what God needs you to do oppose to what you want to do...While promises are continuously fulfilled.

#WDTFIYOURT Challenge

Take a moment to think about anything/everything that you may have promised to someone. Did you fulfill that promise? Or do have an excuse as to why you didn't? If you didn't, put yourself in the shoes of the person that you made the promise to and see how it makes you feel. Before the day is over, seek forgiveness from those that you broke your promise with and forgive those that spoke broken promises to you.

#WDTFIMT Reading/Meditation

- ❑ Proverbs 30
- ❑ 1 Corinthians 1:15-23

Where does this fit in your testimony?

Based on what you read, what is your main take away? And why?

What are you thankful for today? Why?

Who can you do something nice for today? And how?

Study Notes

A Sacrifice of Purpose

There are a lot of things that we have in our lives that we try to hold on to or continuously deal with for whatever reason. Whether it be money, people, material things, careers, etc...we hold on to it. There comes a point where you have to ask yourself what are you willing to sacrifice for the greater purpose of your life? The sacrifice is giving up what makes you feel comfortable, the things that you are used to, the people that you deal with in an unhealthy manner for whatever reason, etc. There are situations that come up in life that will require you to sacrifice something. Not the type of sacrifice that will make you feel that you can bounce back quickly from, but the type of sacrifice that will make you feel you've given something up and you feel the effects of it in your heart, soul, and whole being. The type of sacrifice that only God can give you peace within yourself because if you try to reason with yourself about the sacrifice you'd drive yourself crazy. It's the type of sacrifice that only God can give back to you 100 fold in all ways you would never imagine.

Giving up all excuses of how you feel or the fears you may have...Do you have the guts to let go of anything or everything that can potentially help someone else or prevent your sanity from committing suicide? Are you willing to let go of the people in your life that causes you to have mental heart attacks just so you can be whole...And God can finally move in your life? It can be the littlest thing or situation that you need to decide what are you willing to sacrifice in order for your "Big Picture" to be completly painted right before your eyes.

#WDTFIMT Moment

When I look back over the years, I have truly wanted for nothing. These past few months have put me in a place of sacrifice in all aspects of my life - more than ever before. As many "self" moments that I've had during that time, I've realized that the more I give, get rid of, or let go of (Financially, Relationship-Wise, Career Wise, etc.) it's all for a bigger purpose. Whether if it's with finances, things, or even people...It's allowing me to make room for what is really reserved for me in life and to also deposit into the lives that mean the most at the moment.

#WDTFIYOURT Challenge

I challenge you to follow the urges to give more to your purpose and to get rid of the people/things that are holding you back. It may hurt or put a strain on things in some kind of way, but when it's a matter of life or death regarding your purpose and who is truly meant to be a part of your life...You can't afford to live as a vegetable - merely surviving on the artificial ventilators in your life.

#WDTFIMT Reading/Meditation

- ❏ Job 42
- ❏ Ruth 1

Where does this fit in your testimony?

_____

_____

_____

_____

_____

_____

Based on what you read, what is your main take away? And why?

_____

_____

_____

_____

_____

What are you thankful for today? Why?

_____

_____

_____

Who can you do something nice for today? And how?

_____

_____

_____

_____

Study Notes

A Purposed Delay

Patience...A lot of people know the meaning of the word, but most can say they don't exhibit the word's meaning at all times. I know I'm guilty of it at times. I like to get things done as soon as possible if I know that they need to be done. But when it comes to the things that you want to happen or need to happen it's a whole different ball game when things are out of your control. Another thing to consider is when something comes up that delays a process or delays something from happening...for example traffic delaying your commute or someone taking forever to get back to you on a job application you submitted.

In one instance, the things we want to happen or need to happen are delayed for a purpose. Maybe it's not the right time. Or maybe we have to learn something during the waiting period. Looking at it from a different angle, there may be something delaying the process of something happening. Maybe there was traffic to prevent you from being in the 5 car pileup that happened 2 miles in front of you. Or maybe your resume got lost in the shuffle so it can appear at the right time for you to receive a job offer that you would never imagine. Better yet, in light of it being 9/11 look at how many people that were delayed from getting to work only for their lives to be spared. There is a purpose in everything, even in the delay of things.

#WDTFIMT Moment

When I look at the things I want or need, I've learned to become more patient - something I haven't perfected and sometimes it's evident when I'm getting impatient. When something delays the process of something happening, I do have to admit that it's irritating but when I have to look at the bigger picture I find a reason why the delay can be a good thing. Now...in the process of all if this I still have to know when to delay things on my end. People always think that God is the one to halt things, but there are some things that we have to be mature enough to delay on our own. If not, we'd end up with something that we may not have bargained for. Not everything is meant to be done in the timing that we feel it should be done. That sounds like BLAH BLAH BLAH at times BUT it is sometimes required of us. Even I have to remember that at times....

#WDTFIYOURT Challenge

What has God called to a halt? What are some things that you need to delay willingly? Write down ways you can get past this moment and still be thankful.

#WDTFIMT Reading/Meditation

☐ Isaiah 55

Where does this fit in your testimony?

_____

_____

_____

_____

Based on what you read, what is your main take away? And why?

_____

_____

_____

_____

_____

What are you thankful for today? Why?

_____

_____

_____

Who can you do something nice for today? And how?

_____

_____

_____

_____

Study Notes

_____
_____
_____
_____
_____
_____
_____
_____
_____
_____
_____
_____
_____
_____
_____
_____
_____
_____
_____
_____
_____
_____
_____
_____
_____
_____
_____
_____
_____
_____

A Vulnerable Reluctance

Vulnerability...Something that doesn't come natural to most and also something that most would choose to ignore. Me...I would most definitely choose to ignore any chance to be vulnerable if I can. Not only that, the word does not really exist in my vocabulary. But for all reasons, these past few months, the score has been Vulnerability (A Gazillion Points) vs. Eb (A 0.0000002 Point). We are not going to go through every moment of how I've only won a 0.0000002 point...Just know it has been an internal war with self. When you think of the things you've been through in life, especially with people, you'd ask yourself "Why Bother?" You'd fulfill your role as a "good citizen," but to allow yourself to be vulnerable that won't happen.

I bet if you look at 5 people in your life you would have a list of a million reasons as to why you would never be vulnerable with them...and they may have never done anything wrong to you. It could've been another group of 5 that did something wrong to you. People will always be who they are. You can't change them, but God can if they allow Him to. Keep in mind THEY have to allow Him. YOU have no part in that unless God uses you somehow along their process of change. And to be quite frank with you...It's none of your business if they do change or not. Just focus on what God has for you even if it is a matter of you being vulnerable. It is at those moments that you truly function in purpose and receive whatever God has for you. Don't get it twisted and do it just to receive something from God. Do it because you know what's best for you.

#WDTFIMT Moment

In as many tantrums I may have with God about doing something that I know I'm called to do or allowing myself to let someone "in" my life (that would somehow make me more vulnerable than what I am already)...I remind myself that my trust is always in God (should always be in Him) and not in another human being. If it's in God's will, then the human beings attached to my life (at any given moment) would line up accordingly in some kind of way...if that makes sense.

Being vulnerable allows you to get away from self and to see life situations of self/others from a different point of view. Being vulnerable puts you in a place to depend on God as if there is nothing else to do. The reality is when you think about that statement...There really isn't anything else to do but depend on Him.

#WDTFIYOURT Challenge

What do you need to depend on God for more often? How has it worked for you not doing so? In what ways do you need to be more vulnerable? Be honest, with yourself, when you answer these questions.

#WDTFIMT Reading/Meditation

- ❏ Job 8
- ❏ Psalm 37

Where does this fit in your testimony?

_____
_____
_____
_____
_____

Based on what you read, what is your main take away? And why?

_____
_____
_____
_____
_____

What are you thankful for today? Why?

_____
_____
_____

Who can you do something nice for today? And how?

_____
_____
_____
_____
_____
_____
_____

Study Notes

Wants vs. Needs

Grocery shopping, nowadays, has turned into a list of what my household actually needs and not what we want. When you shop for what you need and not what you want, you're more than likely to be conscience of the money you spend along with the type of food you eat. What would happen if you looked at life the same way? What would happen if you start to take inventory of how much time you are spending on things/people that aren't worth it? What would happen if you start to look at your wants vs. your needs in life and you realize that what you want would actually cause more headaches than your needs? What would happen if you completely stopped fascinating on your wants and allow God to work on what you need amongst everything else He has for you?

#WDTFIMT Moment

I have to be one to admit that amongst planning things day by day I tend to plan things in life. Some are things that I need to do while some are what I want to do. Within these past few months, I have been challenged in all areas to just let go and let God. Let go of my wants of being able to be a stay at home mom. Let go of my wants for wanting to have more kids and being in a union more than just a marriage. (Yes...I said a union of more than just a marriage. That's another topic.) Let go of my wants within my career. Let go of my wants in everything. Once I let go...My eyes opened to all possibilities of life even though everything has not been made visible to me. Is any of that easy? Ummmmm...Nope. Still is a work in progress to be honest. I don't throw myself on the floor, in protest, as much as I used to.

It comes to a point, in life, when you look at the needs of others and how you may fit into the puzzles of their life. There comes a point in life when you have to know that God is working on everything on your behalf. Even if you don't know everything He's doing or has already done, you just have to trust that He knows what is best for you. I can't lie and say there are times when I see babies that my heart doesn't melt and I don't get urges of buying a puppy to fill a void. I can't lie and say that I don't feel guilty for not being able to be at home to raise my kids fulltime. I can't lie about a lot of things. What I can say is at this point in my lifetime my needs are far greater than my wants and hopefully when you get to a point in realizing that (if you haven't already)...You will be able to see all of the unseen possibilities for your life as well.

#WDTFIYOURT Challenge

What is it that you want versus what you need? Write a list and determine if each item is truly something that is designed by God to be a part of your life.

For the items that you know that are not designed for God's purpose, pray that you can see why and accept the answer as to why.

#WDTFIMT Reading/Meditation

- ❑ Philippians 4
- ❑ Matthew 6:5-14

Where does this fit in your testimony?

Based on what you read, what is your main take away? And why?

What are you thankful for today? Why?

Who can you do something nice for today? And how?

Study Notes

Steps Ahead

In all things, I usually try to plan ahead. Things needed for the house, finances, meals, driving time, meetings, etc. Everyone who knows me, besides communication, organization is something this is of importance to me. Without it, in some things, I end up feeling like I have OCD or that I can't function fully. I can say that I'm sometimes guilty of planning ahead so much that I never leave any room for error. Ultimately meaning that I may plan something and expect for it to go the way that it was planned. I laugh as I think of it because my life, these past few months, has been nothing like that. In some areas of my life...Yes. BUT in all areas...NO. It's very evident in the areas that are close to home and heart - especially when God has challenged me even more to relinquish control of my heart and life in most aspects. Nothing that I'm complaining about, but it proves to me that there are some things that happen - whether if you pray about them or not...Ultimately you (I) still have to remember that all along that you (I) are planning steps ahead, God has planned way further than we may have even thought to do - all for us to know/learn (eventually) that even in the planning of our lives we can't keep God in a box.

#WDTFIMT Moment

It may sometimes feel that God is playing charades or scavenger hunt with certain things pertaining to life...But when you ultimately make it a point to be still and release whatever situation it is that has come up things are bound to work out. One thing to never let go of is that childlike faith...God will always work something out whether if you planned for it to come up or not. Another thing to take into consideration is that as we pray for things God may answer but don't expect to plan the answer for Him. It's all about His will and not ours. As you remind yourself of that, know that I'm having to do the same.

#WDTFIYOURT Challenge

Go a whole week without planning something and ask God to lead you. As you go throughout the week, write down everything that comes to your mind.

#WDTFIMT Reading/Meditation

- ❑ Deuteronomy 31
- ❑ Psalm 17

Where does this fit in your testimony?

_____

_____

_____

_____

_____

_____

Based on what you read, what is your main take away? And why?

_____

_____

_____

_____

_____

_____

What are you thankful for today? Why?

_____

_____

_____

_____

Who can you do something nice for today? And how?

_____

_____

_____

_____

_____

_____

_____

Study Notes

To Speak or Not To Speak

If you were to ask a group of people what the word "Communication" meant to them, you'd most probably get a gazillion different answers. Although there is a true meaning of communication, a lot of people see it differently. When you look at the ways people communicate, you have to take into consideration their mindset, upbringing, blah, blah, blah. So when you have something to really say, you may have to step back and take all of those factors into consideration so you can truly be heard. Should you have to do that every time...I think you should if you truly care about being heard effectively and really care about the person that you are "communicating" with. So what do you do when you know something needs to be said and the best thing to do is to not say anything at all??? As much as that would be a personal battle, some things are best left unsaid until the time is right or until the situation actually works itself out. How many times have you been in a situation when you've said something that was rightful to say BUT it was said at the wrong time? How many relationships are faced with communication issues because of point of views, bad timing of saying things, etc., etc., etc.?

#WDTFIMT Moment

For many who know me...I'm a real stickler for communication. BUT if I'm put in a position where I eventually feel that I can't express myself in a way that is to be heard fairly, uninterrupted, or anything else...I'll just back down and go into "Dude Mode". That's one thing that I can admit to. Is it always right? Maybe not, but that's my way of backing off and just letting things be what they are especially since I know my mouth can kill someone before a gun does. Not only that...I just hate going back and forth about stuff. What's the point? To me...if the person truly wanted to hear what needed to be said they would listen before speaking. That is why we all have 2 ears and 1 mouth (God knew what He was doing). Unless there is a discussion to resolve the matter effectively...Mum's the word on my end. There have been a few situations that have come up this week where I had the right to say something, but in actuality the things I had to consider was timing, would the other person just be stuck in their way of point of views, etc., etc. It eventually gets to a point where it does get frustrating, especially when dealing with people you really care about. BUT, in actuality, that is a moment for you to move out of your own way and allow God to do what He needs to do. It gets to a point where you have to pray "God regardless if I'm right, let the other person see it from YOUR point of view and not MINE." Don't get it twisted...as you say those words you may be clenching your teeth and there may be an "adjustment" period for you to even have a conversation with that person, but if you do it your way where would you really end up in the situation? Let that be an opportunity to also work on self – there is always room for it. Always remember to walk in love regardless and just hope for the best regardless of how you feel. It may not feel all cozy and comfy at first…but it would be worth it in the long run. Just something to think about, before you say anything regardless if you are right. Believe me…I'm in that position right now.

#WDTFIYOURT Challenge

Think of a situation that you are currently going through. Without thinking of who is right or wrong, look at the situation from God's point of view. Who is right or wrong now?

#WDTFIMT Reading/Meditation

- ❏ James 13
- ❏ Psalm 31

Where does this fit in your testimony?

_____

_____

_____

_____

_____

Based on what you read, what is your main take away? And why?

_____

_____

_____

_____

_____

What are you thankful for today? Why?

_____

_____

_____

Who can you do something nice for today? And how?

_____

_____

_____

_____

_____

_____

Study Notes

Life

There are things that come up in life that we sometimes may not understand and if we do understand we usually question when that particular situation will pass. As we watch the news, we can see the craziness that is taking place in the lives of others...Thanking God that it is not us who is experiencing that news story but also having sympathy for those who are. An atheist is quick to say that "If there is truly a God in Heaven then why do bad things happen to good people?" What those atheists do not understand is the personal protection that God has for His children. What they also do not understand is that God's love, grace, and forgiveness is worth more than all the money and things of this world.

#WDTFIMT Moment

There are a few people in my life that are really going through a lot of challenges. So much in a way, that my prayer life and thoughts have not been focused on self. I always knew that part of my gift is prayer/encouragement. BUT as I continually walk in that gift I am being put through a purging process. Is it comfortable at all times...No. Even as I'm given things to write, I question "Who is even going to read this?" But really at this moment, it's not about what I question it's about what I'm told to do.

#WDTFIYOURT Challenge

If you are going through something in life, as some of my loved ones are...Just throw up your hands and praise God for how AWESOME He is. Speak to your situation because God has given you dominion over EVERYTHING. Ask God to forgive you of everything big and small and make it a point to follow His instructions. He has not given you a spirit of fear, but He's given you the spirit of love, power, and a peaceful mind. He has already declared you His child so walk in your birthright and proudly say that NO weapon formed against you shall prosper. He has already taken care of anything that you may be going through so know to count it all joy. His ways are not your ways and His thoughts are not your thoughts. He has already done everything exceedingly, abundantly...far more than you can ever ask or think. Declare that today is the last day that you will ever question God and what is going on in your life. Declare that today is a day that you will stop focusing on self and be used as God sees fit because He has already taken care of EVERYTHING. Just say that over and over until it reaches past your mind and into your heart. Things could be worse but God has already given you a promise that things will get better. You are more than a conqueror in your situation...So don't just act like it walk in your victory!

#WDTFIMT Reading/Meditation

- ❑ Psalm 119
- ❑ 1 Thessalonians 5:12-22

Where does this fit in your testimony?

_____

_____

_____

_____

Based on what you read, what is your main take away? And why?

_____

_____

_____

_____

_____

What are you thankful for today? Why?

_____

_____

_____

Who can you do something nice for today? And how?

_____

_____

_____

_____

Study Notes

God's Friction

A couple of days ago one of my kids decided to wash clothes without checking to see if there was anything in the pockets of all clothes. SOOOOO...once the clothes came out the dryer they were colorfully decorated in the BRIGHTEST blue crayon color that Crayola has ever created. Off course I freaked out and I actually I cried for a good while. Today I stood in my laundry with every Oxiperioxidestainremover cleaner I could get my hands on. I felt like I was creating the next must-have laundry detergent. As I scrubbed I saw the light at the end of the tunnel...UNTIL I turned over each garment to find more spots that needed to be scrubbed. The friction between my hands and the clothes began to make my hands hurt, burn, and everything else all at the same time. Needless to say, after 2 shirts, 2 skirts, and 3 pairs of pants, I got out most of what I can (praying that as I do a pre-soak before a full wash that all will be well). I have 2 more pairs of pants that may not make it out of the soaking ICU that I created in my kitchen sink. That's how bad they are, but it's worth the try.

WDTFIMT Moment

As I scrubbed and scrubbed, I began to think of what friction does. It causes some type of reaction. Then I began to think about God's friction - the nudges or gestures He gives us when He is trying to get our attention. Not only that, God's friction is a process that we go through when we need to be purged for His purpose. It's not always comfortable. It's not always desirable. We are like the stained clothes. Some parts of us may be clean or repaired but when we are flipped over or turned inside out there are still some spots that God needs to continue working on within us. Regardless of where you are today in life, know that as uncomfortable the process you are experiencing may be...It's for a glorious purpose and you will win in the long run.

#WDTFIYOURT Challenge

Allow yourself to be soaked in God's perfect soap. There are so many things that we feel as we go through any uncomfortable process. Write down all feelings that come to you and be honest. The only way to get past this stage in your life is to be honest with yourself and God.

#WDTFIMT Reading/Meditation

- ❏ Daniel 12
- ❏ Psalm 19

Where does this fit in your testimony?

Based on what you read, what is your main take away? And why?

What are you thankful for today? Why?

Who can you do something nice for today? And how?

Study Notes

Stop Asking "Why?"

Who, what, when, where, and why...Most of us are familiar with the book report standards from our earlier years. As we get older those standards still apply in some kind of way as we deal with everyday life. I think as we face trouble or trials within our lives we tend to focus on the "Why?" more than anything else. "Why is this happening to me?"..."Why do I keep going through the same things?" The "Why?s" go on and on. You can even become overwhelmed with the "Why?s" of other people...especially when you are close to them. When we become consumed with the "Why?s" we tend to lose sight of everything else we need to look at.

#WDTFIMT Moment

I have to admit these past few days have been a challenge. In a quiet moment yesterday, I got a reminder to start asking "How?"

"How do I get through a specific moment or situation?"

"How do I stay encouraged for myself and those around me?"

As much as I have known this, I still needed to be reminded. When you start asking "How?" the "Why?" becomes minute. When you start asking "How?" the "What?s" that you need in life are manifested. When you start asking "How?" the "Where?s" become revealed on where you need to be or go (Spiritually/Physically) to resolve your "Why?s". When you start asking "How?" the "Who?s" can be placed in your life to either help with your "Why?s"...or you just may end helping that "Who?" with their "Why?s". The "Who?s" that are sincere and really care about you will remain in your life regardless of what comes up. In all...you may know or never know "Why?" It may be something that you've gotten yourself into being hard headed or it may be something that you still haven't passed as a test or it may be something that you need to do that you've ignored. The reason can be anything depending on where you are in life...BUT you can always be assured that the "When?" will happen when God sees fit. You just have to trust His "How?s", "What?s", "Where?s", "Who?s" and also His "Why?s"...even when it doesn't make sense.

#WDTFIYOURT Challenge

What do you need to stop questioning God on? Go a whole week without questioning God and see what answers you get.

#WDTFIMT Reading/Meditation

- ❑ Ezekiel 18
- ❑ 1 Kings 10

Where does this fit in your testimony?

_____

_____

_____

_____

_____

_____

Based on what you read, what is your main take away? And why?

_____

_____

_____

_____

_____

_____

What are you thankful for today? Why?

_____

_____

_____

Who can you do something nice for today? And how?

_____

_____

_____

_____

Study Notes

I Don't Want To Grow Up!

For many of us that grew up in the late 70s and all of the 80s are quite familiar with the infamous Toys R Us chant..."I don't want to grow...I want to be a Toys R Us Kid!" That was true to heart for all of us that wanted to play with toys, be outside all day, and not be bothered with life. BUT then we began to see life differently and began to moan during our pre-teens and teen years..."I can't wait to be an adult!" We merely said that out of disgust with the many rules that were hung over our heads. Ironically as adults, we're quick to tell children to cherish their childhood years as we secretly kick and scream..."I don't want to be an adult!" When it's all said and done we do have a choice whether if we grow up or not. Regardless of what decision we make consequences (good or bad) will follow.

#WDTFIMT Moment

This may be the longest #WDTFIMT Moment that I've ever written...but I have to get it done. There has been A LOT going on these past few months. Some great things that I can only give thanks for. And other things...I can only look in God's "face" and say "Seriously...I'm supposed to be the adult in ALL of this???" I'm speaking of the situations where you feel that you're tapped out and you have given everything your all. The situations where you smile regardless of it feeling as if there is a dagger in your heart. The situations where you are standing on God's promises to only feel as if you've let down walls and your guard for nothing. The situations where you can just go off on someone and not even regret the words that you may speak because you want them to feel your pain as they have hurt you. The list of situations goes on and on. I keep hearing in those moments that it's time to grow up regardless of what comes your way...But it's still a choice to do so.

Choice #1 – Close your ears to what you've been hearing about growing up and continue to have tantrums. One thing to learn about God is...He doesn't respond to any tantrum episodes that we may have in life. He pays attention to the things you say to Him in anger. He pays attention to the self-pity parties you give yourself on a regular basis. And He also marks every word that you may say as if you're bigger and badder than He is with your "I don't care" attitude. He pays attention...BUT He never responds. He may give you a nudge here and there, but for as long as you keep ignoring His nudges He'll eventually back off. He leaves you to your jacked up attitude, while He waits patiently for you to see that how you have decided to handle things was really the wrong choice. You can't walk in purpose with this choice. You can't walk in victory with this choice. With this choice, you live a completely DEFEATED life. And why? Because you made that choice.

Choice #2 - Take refuge in the secret place of the Most High. As things come your way, trust that God will bring you through. Look back on all things that He has done and just imagine all that He will continue to do. Be the adult that He's called you to be regardless of what comes your way and walk in Love/Faith/Forgiveness. Whether if you realize it or not...It's that simple. It may not be easy but it's that simple.

I can't say that I've never decided Choice #1 in life because I have...but it ultimately becomes more tiresome than it would be making the 2nd Choice. There are so many things that we are able to see in the midst of a storm if we choose to grow up. And that's speaking on not only growing up as an adult but also growing up within God. He knows that things won't be easy at times way before we even encounter them, so why can we just not grow up and trust that He'll see us through. Many of us shouldn't be alive today, but the same God that has protected us, years back, still allows us to breathe today and I know He's not doing it for nothing.

One thing that is pressed upon me is purpose. What I need to do rather than what I want to do. I have a lot of talents, but there are specific things that I need to do in regards to my purpose. For example, these WDTFIMT Moments have to get done. These entries are the smallest thing that I'm told to do...but sometimes I'm not feeling it when I'm told to do them. And I have to admit there are moments when I'm told to do bigger things and I look God in His face and say "Dude...Seriously I've gone above and beyond than what you told me to do and you want me to do what???" You know you have a purpose when you go on strike from GOD, Inc. and you have NO peace. You know you have a purpose when you're being pushed out of your comfort zone to go above and beyond than normal. There are A LOT of things that I've submitted my two-week notice on, but because I need the peace and protection of God I eventually have that meeting of being "rehired". I not only need His peace and protection, but I need ALL that He promised me as His child spiritually, mentally, emotionally, etc. And after that "rehiring" meeting, I'm always told there is a "project" for me to handle. Regardless of what excuse I come up with I know it's inevitable that I would lose that battle...So why not just be an adult and walk in purpose? I have to forget all that is going on around me, no matter how painful it may be, and just continue to walk in purpose.

There may be a lot of you that may have made the 1st choice. And with that choice, you are stuck at the deep end of an abyss. I encourage you, today, to truly realize that your purpose is bigger than you. Everything that you're going through is a test and can also be a distraction. What we don't realize is that we can say the simplest thing as "I don't care" and before we realize it our situations become way worse than what they started to be or we become more distant from God, the people that love us, and most importantly from self.

#WDTFIYOURT Challenge

Find a moment today to just let go of the tantrums and trust that God has your back. Your purpose was designed by God and He already knows what needs to be done for you to fulfill your purpose...so why not trust Him? Your purpose isn't only for your benefit. It is to be a benefit of those around you and many more that God would send down your path. If you're unsure of your purpose, then ask for a clear understanding of what you need to do. The longer you delay the inevitable the more you'll be playing Russian roulette with not only your destiny, but also with your life. Tomorrow is never promised. Not even the very next second that you read this is promised.

#WDTFIMT Reading/Meditation

- ❑ Psalm 23
- ❑ James 1:21-27

Where does this fit in your testimony?

Based on what you read, what is your main take away? And why?

What are you thankful for today? Why?

Who can you do something nice for today? And how?

Study Notes

Do You Need a Heart Massage?

Massages are known to not only loosen up tensed muscles, but it is also known to detox your body from whatever toxins you may have accumulated. It may not get rid of everything, but it does help the detox process. Why do you think any masseuse always encourages us to drink a lot of water after getting a massage?

#WDTFIMT Moment

For some reason as I was driving this morning, I kept telling myself I need to get a massage. And as I kept telling myself that I needed to get a massage, I then began to realize that I did not need a body massage...I need to get a heart massage. I realized that when I felt my heart getting tensed about something that I am dealing with. Something that would make you cock your head and say "Seriously???" When you look at the things that you hold dear to heart, you know there are just some things that people shouldn't mess with or be considered as a threat towards. If they mess with the matters of your heart or become a threat, you have a whole different mindset altogether. Your heart not only becomes tensed, but your heart becomes toxic with bitterness, unforgiveness, etc.

At what point do you realize that you need a heart massage? You realize you need a heart massage when you are tempted to kill someone with your words without thinking twice because of how they have made you feel or something that they have done to you. You realize that you need a heart massage when you can't even pray in a way for God to hear you because your heart is so heavy from whatever you may be dealing with. You realize you need a heart massage when all thoughts towards a person or situation are not lining up with what you know need to think. The list goes on.

When I tell you life and people can make you want to say "Why bother?"...You'd be tempted to say it more so when you are being pushed to get a heart massage. Just as in any massage, a heart massage doesn't always feel so great. There are moments when you feel pressure and all you can do is cry out silently in pain because you know you cannot escape the toxic purging process. There are moments when your heart is being stretched and tugged in every direction in order for your heart to be softened while releasing any tension. There may be moments when you are being told to relax, but because the pain is so unbearable you hold in your breath praying that the pain will pass and you'll live through it. There are moments when you may feel the kneading of God's hands so heavy on your heart that all you can do is surrender anything and everything in order to experience relief.

A major step for most of us is the acknowledgment of us needing a heart massage. The question ultimately ends up to be...How soon will we make our appointment with the Heart Masseuse?

#WDTFIYOURT Challenge

If you were to create a detox for your heart, what would it consist of and why? What "toxins" abide in your heart that you know need to be released?

#WDTFIMT Reading/Meditation

- ❏ Genesis 6
- ❏ Proverbs 15

Where does this fit in your testimony?

_____

_____

_____

_____

_____

Based on what you read, what is your main take away? And why?

_____

_____

_____

_____

_____

What are you thankful for today? Why?

_____

_____

_____

Who can you do something nice for today? And how?

_____

_____

_____

_____

_____

_____

Study Notes

Spiritual Vomit

Have you ever wondered why people vomit? Sidebar…I may need to put a disclaimer out there on this one. I don't know how graphic-sensitive some of you may be, especially if you're a visual person.

DISCLAIMER: This entry may or may not make your face screw up.

Soooo…Going back to the question. Have you ever wondered why people vomit? People vomit when their body automatically rejects something that is toxic. Here is more of why a person would vomit (Thanks to Google and Friends):

Vomiting is a bodily reflex against harmful substances that you may eat or ingest. If something toxin gets into your digestive track, which is anything from your esophagus all the way through your stomach, intestines, and out through your butt, your body will upchuck as an attempt purge them from your body. If you didn't have this kind of defense mechanism then anything harmful in your system could easily get absorbed through your small intestine.

Vomiting is an involuntary reaction that happens without you having to conscientiously think about it. It's controlled by a part of the brain called the medulla oblongata. This same part of the brain controls other involuntary functions like breathing and heartbeat. When your body decides it needs to get rid of something with the old heave-ho, the medulla oblongata sends a message to your digestive track that it should begin reverse peristalsis. Peristalsis is a series of contractions in your GI track that helps move food through your body. The reverse of this causes you to vomit, purging yourself of any toxins in your system.

#WDTFIMT Moment

Most of you who know me automatically knows that if I was bleeding internally…I would still find a way to get things done. With that being said…I have been dealing with a very bad case of food poisoning these past few days. How did it all start? On Tuesday…When I wanted some fried fish. I don't know if it was the fish or the tartar sauce, but either way, I ended up feeling more than green in the face. Today is Saturday and I'm just getting to a point of feeling better.

Since Tuesday my stomach's world has been turned upside down and flipped inside out. After eating the fish, I felt fine. BUT later that night I felt as if I wanted to hide under my bed from the Vomit Monster. I don't like to throw up. You couldn't pay me a million dollars to throw up. I'm that serious about it. Nonetheless...I lost that battle while me and the bathroom sink, toilet, the funny tasting pink stuff, and everything else became one. I threw up everything I ate that day...even what I ate before the fish.

Amazing how our bodies are smart enough to reject the things that are not meant to stay within us. It's just something to never try to figure out since God created us and with that, He is awesome just for it. I began to look at this from a spiritual aspect...oddly as my vomit stared back at me and I wanted to fall over on the bathroom floor. Have you ever noticed that as you become more mature in the things of God, that your Spirit Man can only stomach but so much? There are just certain things that we can tolerate spiritually as we begin to seek God more on our purpose and His will for our lives. Certain things no longer become entertaining. Certain things no longer become enjoyable. Certain people that we used to be around no longer become worthy of our time. Think about it. As we grow within God, our Spirit Man lines up with the things that God wants us to experience and see from a spiritual standpoint. BUT how many of us try to hold on to the things that we need to let go of, especially when we know that they are toxic for us. Like me...I don't care how toxic anything is in my body...I REFUSE to throw it up. I refuse to be subjected to becoming victim to the regurgitating process. Even though I know it would make me feel better, I just won't give in.

#WDTFIYOURT Challenge

What is your Spirit Man rejecting that you need to throw up? What has God been talking to you about in regards to what you need to let go of, but you just refuse to let go? He tells us things that are nothing but for the best within our lives. Whatever you need to let go of may be the answer to the drama that you have going on in your life. Whatever you need to let go of may be the answer to blessings that God has been trying to get to you. I don't know what it is that you are dealing with. Just make a point to allow yourself to throw up spiritually. It will do you some good!

#WDTFIMT Reading/Meditation

- ❑ Proverbs 26
- ❑ 2 Chronicles 7:14

Where does this fit in your testimony?

_____

_____

_____

_____

_____

_____

Based on what you read, what is your main take away? And why?

_____

_____

_____

_____

_____

What are you thankful for today? Why?

_____

_____

_____

Who can you do something nice for today? And how?

_____

_____

_____

_____

_____

_____

Study Notes

The Children of FEAR

FEAR…False Evidence Appearing Real. I'm sure everyone is familiar with that saying. How can we not be familiar with it? We can quote it in our sleep, but do we really know what that means. For some reason, there are times in life where we become fearful of something. And the crazy thing is…we are naturally fearful of some things without even being taught to be fearful. We subject ourselves to so many children of FEAR that we sometimes lose ourselves within their make-up – ultimately leaving us helpless and defeated. You may be asking yourself…What do you mean children of FEAR? I'm talking about Anxiety, Depression, Worrying, Insecurity, etc. We all know them so well, but we fail to realize their origin…FEAR.

#WDTFIMT Moment

I asked a group of people to send me a list of things to write about. From the list of topics, that I received, the children of FEAR were popping up left and right so I had to figure out how to write about all of them without becoming redundant…So that is where the Children of FEAR came from. I also had to figure out how to tie this into one of my moments. Honestly, I've suppressed some things these past couple of weeks so much to really evaluate one of these Children of FEAR, specifically for self, is something that I don't know if I can do right now. I think I'm really trying to keep myself at a state of normalcy at this moment…If there is really such a thing of being normal.

When one plays with the children of FEAR, something has happened in his/her life to accept the playdate invitation. Think about it. All of the children of FEAR originates from something that we are afraid of or from something that triggers a reaction so deep within us, we become a prisoner until we call a time out or cut ties with anything that is keeping us hostage.

Worrying and anxiety can pretty much go hand in hand. One can worry so much he/she can experience anxiety attacks. One worries about the what ifs in life. What if this happens? What if that happens? After going through all of the what-ifs, one can then start to question his/herself…ultimately becoming insecure about something. And after becoming insecure about self, an individual then becomes depressed based on everything else that took place within the worryinganxietyinsecure stage. These children of FEAR eventually brings one to a place of darkness in every area of their lives. When one is in a dark place in life, they are barely alive. You may see them walking, talking, etc., but they lose a piece of themselves and it seems as if you're looking at someone dying a slow death because they just don't know how to come to the other side where the light is shining. I've seen someone go through moments as such and it just hurts to even see them that way. No matter how much you encourage that person or try to be there for them, this is just something that you can only pray with your all that they will get past and still be sane after going through all of this.

I don't know who is bogged down with the children of FEAR. I don't know what triggered whatever you are going through, but I can only encourage you to look at what is causing you to go through whatever you are going through. And as you look at what is causing you to FEAR evaluate the following:

Yourself - What are you doing to cause whatever is going on? Do you need to change your outlook on life? Do you need to change the way you think about yourself or life in general? What drama have you caused to even get yourself where you are now?

Your Surroundings – Who or what is causing you to go through what you are going through? What or who do you need to let go of?

Your Solution – What do you need to put in place for you to get past whatever you are going through? What do you have to be honest with self about? What do you have to be honest with God about? What do you need to do to get yourself in a place of being spiritually sound within your heart and your mind?

I'm not saying getting past your situation is going to be easy, but to live in FEAR is like committing suicide – a slow one. That's really the best way that I can put it. FEAR is something that we have to shun away from. Easier said than done…yes I know because I even have to remind myself of what I'm telling you. There are days where I just have to shut down mentally and seek answers spiritually. Maybe that is something that I need to do right now for whatever reason, now that I think about it as I write this…But I challenge you to let go of whatever you don't have control over and allow your FEARs to become the Joy of what God intended you to have.

#WDTFIYOURT Challenge
Answer all questions within the passage. Speak to the FEAR that is holding you hostage and take dominion over it.

#WDTFIMT Reading/Meditation

- ☐ 2 Timothy 1
- ☐ Exodus 20

Where does this fit in your testimony?

_____

_____

_____

_____

_____

_____

Based on what you read, what is your main take away? And why?

_____

_____

_____

_____

_____

_____

What are you thankful for today? Why?

_____

_____

_____

_____

Who can you do something nice for today? And how?

_____

_____

_____

_____

_____

_____

Study Notes

What Is There to Hold On To?

What is there to hold on to? This question came to mind as I was driving one day and saw an insect hanging onto my window for dear life. I used to think that insects get tired and liked to hitch rides whenever possible…But for some reason on this day, I saw something totally different. I saw an insect that would not give up or let go regardless of how fast I was driving – especially since the speed (not to mention how fast I was driving) could actually cost its life. The faster I went the more the insect struggled. I think it actually lost a wing.

Seeing that insect go through what it went through, I started to think about what we actually go through in the same sense…Holding on to something when whatever it is that we are holding on to can actually cost us something in life. Nine times out of ten not being worth it. There are so many areas in our lives that we know that we can benefit from a re-evaluation period to figure out what there really is to hold on to. I, myself, have gone through these moments quite often, especially during times that seem as if things are at a standstill or during times of frustration. So ask yourself…What is there to hold on to?

Broken Promises or Being Hurt by Someone

- The promise was never fulfilled so why hold on to the fact that someone let you down?
- A person can never truly love you if they do not know how to…so why hold on?
- You can't force anyone to love you…so why hold on?

Your Past

- Your past is your past so why hold on especially if you made it a point to move on in life?

Your Hang Ups

- Why should other people suffer because of your hang-ups?

Relationships (Business and Personal)

- Is the person really worth it?
- What value does the person add to your life and to your purpose?
- Do you deal with this person out of fear of the unknown in life?

- Can this person really accept you for who you are and expect nothing else?
- Are you equally yoked with this person in all aspects of your life?
- Is this person in your life because of your will or God's will?

Operating Outside of Your Purpose

- You are gifted to do a lot of things...But what is it that you should be doing that you're not?
- How many degrees will you pursue in life just to feel fulfilled?
- How many corporate ladders will you climb just for a title and validation?
- Why keep running on the hamster wheel that doesn't get you anywhere?

The list of evaluation areas and questions can keep going on and on...But only you can determine the areas that need to be evaluated in your life.

#WDTFIYOURT Challenge

Answer all questions within this passage. Take your time to reflect on each answer and seek God as you do.

#WDTFIMT Reading/Meditation

- ❏ Jeremiah 24
- ❏ 1 Peter 4

Where does this fit in your testimony?

Based on what you read, what is your main take away? And why?

What are you thankful for today? Why?

Who can you do something nice for today? And how?

Study Notes

Walk on Water in the Bathtub

I sent out a #WDTFIMT Nugget that stated…"If Jesus walked on water in the ocean…You can walk on water in the bathtub. I dare you to do it." I know some of you may have read that nugget and asked yourself "Why walk on water in the bathtub?" As most of you may have been focused on the bathtub, you may not have realized that I said Jesus walked on water in the ocean, when He really walked on water in the sea. With that said…Let me back track and tell you how all of this bathtub stuff got started.

#WDTFIMT Moment

Monday was a VERY rainy day. I was walking towards the store with the kids and I saw my son walking towards a HUGE puddle deliberately. The first thing that came out of my mouth was, "You better not walk in that puddle unless you're going to walk on water like Jesus." Of course, he asked me if I was serious. What do you think I said? Yes…I was dead serious. Some may question why I would even say something to spark something "unusual" within the mind of an 11-year-old boy. For those who know me, I tend to spark a lot of things within any given situation. As we entered the store, the questions started to roll. Here's the conversation:

Son: So you mean to tell me Jesus really walked on water?

Me: Yup

Son: How did He walk on water?

Me: With his legs, faith, and authority.

Son: How can I walk on water?

Me: In faith and authority.

Son: So if someone was drowning in the deep part of the ocean…Would you swim or walk on water?

Me: Walk on water.

Son: Why would you do that?

Me: Because if the person is already in the deep, that would be the only way for me to get to them without drowning myself. Not only that, I would need to preserve my strength to carry the person back and I would be too tired to do that if I swam in the ocean.

LONG MOMENT OF SILENCE....

Son: So if I filled up the bathtub with water...I can walk on it?

Me: Yup...As long as you clean up any mess you make on the bathroom floor while walking on water.

That's an everyday, normal conversation that I have with my kids. Most would think I have lost my mind for doing so, but that is where people limit themselves within the faith and authority that they are granted to operate in. Why did I say Jesus walked on water in the ocean? I said it because Jesus is bigger than anything and if He needed to walk on water in the ocean, then He has the authority to do so. No different than me telling my son he has authority to walk on water in the bathtub. And with that said, I know that if my son has enough faith to walk on water in the bathtub...Then why would he be afraid to walk on water in the ocean? The only difference would be is that the bathtub is in a familiar place within my home. The ocean is a different story. The ocean is a big body of water that seems to be unfamiliar and never ending if you are in the middle - especially in the midst of a storm. BUT if you decide to walk on water in faith and your God-given authority, why would it even matter if you are in the ocean or in the bathtub? It shouldn't.

It's been on my heart this week to challenge your faith deficiencies...Including mine. There are things that you need to accomplish in life and God is telling you to walk on water, but you are comfortable sitting on the toilet in the bathroom. You're not only sitting on the toilet, but you are stuck there out of comfort. There are areas that many of us have become comfortable in and we wonder why things seem to be stagnant or full of confusion/drama. I don't know what you are dealing with, but you do. God may have told you to start a ministry, but you continuously flush any/every opportunity down the toilet. God may have told you to give up something so He can replace it with something even better...but instead you are holding onto that very thing and it is as irritating as cardboard toilet tissue. God may have told you to just simply fill up the tub, but because of the fear you walk in you just let the water run without putting the stopper in the tub so it can fill up. How can you ever walk on water in the bathtub if you can't even fill up the tub with faith and authority?

#WDTFIYOURT Challenge

I challenge you, this week, to walk on water in faith and authority...LITERALLY. I dare you to. If you do, send me the video so it can be used as a testimony of encouragement for others. I will do the same!

#WDTFIMT Reading/Meditation

❑ Mark 6

Where does this fit in your testimony?

_____

_____

_____

_____

_____

_____

Based on what you read, what is your main take away? And why?

_____

_____

_____

_____

_____

_____

What are you thankful for today? Why?

_____

_____

_____

_____

Who can you do something nice for today? And how?

_____

_____

_____

_____

_____

_____

_____

Study Notes

Status: DNR

DNR...That is what kept coming to mind so many times this weekend for whatever reason. I guess I've been thinking about life and some situations in my life. My grandmother came to mind as well. Her status is DNR. For those that do not know what DNR stands for...It means "Do Not Resuscitate".

Many people have the DNR status. For whatever reason, at the moment of a life-threatening emergency, they just want to die and not be helped. They do not want anyone to perform CPR. They do not want to get shocked with those electrical thingamjingies. Knowing this, one would question are they playing God in their own lives...But another can argue if those that help a dying person are trying to play God as well. That would be a discussion to have at a later time. I also like to look at DNR as...Do Not Resurrect.

#WDTFIMT Moment

I haven't declared my DNR status in life or death situation, but I have to be real and say that I have declared DNR in some situations in my life. One situation in particular...God and I have had some very interesting convos about. One where I'm left with my arms folded and lips pouting, but I know not to cross God nor the authority that He has in my life.

God: I need you to do this for this person.
Me: Would it even matter to this person...DNR

God: I need you to intercede for this person.
Me: It's 3 in the morning...DNR

God: I need you to show your heart to this person.
Me: I've shown my heart. I've even given away the key and this is where things are now...DNR

God: I have a word. I need you to say this to this person.
Me: What I say wouldn't mean a hill of beans and how will they know it's You and not me...DNR

God: I need you to realize that regardless of what you deem as DNR...Needs to be raised from the dead because there is a work to be done not just with you, but with this person as well.

Long Pause
Long Pause Again

Me: OK....

How many of us has had those conversations? How many of us have a situation in our lives where we plastered DNR all over it?

Possible Situations...

Relationships – Whether if it is a friendship or a marriage, some of us have been so hurt and we quickly say DNR. We do not want to deal with the pain, the emotions, and anything else that would make us feel as if we have lost our mind. If you're anything like me, I end up putting up my walls and dealing with things with a business frame of mind. I guess it's easy for me to deal with things that way...it's a sense of having control now that I think of it. But what is God saying about a specific relationship that you've been dealing with? That person may have hurt you or disappointed you, but what did God instill in you that this particular person needs to see. What word or act of kindness is God pushing you to give so that person can see God for who He is?

Your Purpose – Many of us live life without fulfilling our true purpose. There are things that happen in life and we use the excuse of getting "sidetracked" or we just live in plain rebellion/ignorance. We know that there is a bigger purpose in which we are to live in, but we make excuses not to do so. We use our past as an excuse. We use other people as an excuse. Whatever excuse we use, we tell God DNR. DNR the fire that He instilled in us. DNR the passion that He has given us towards His will. DNR the visions that He's shown us over and over.

I'm sure there are other areas that we can analyze and that will take all day, but I'm sure you get what I'm saying. As I prepared to write this, I wondered what if Jesus told God DNR (Do Not Resurrect) as He was being crucified on the cross? That is something to truly think about. Jesus being crucified was one thing, but He being raised from the dead was something totally different. So imagine what situations in your life are to serve as a major purpose after being raised from the dead? Who are we to tell God...DNR???

#WDTFIYOURT Challenge

Take a sheet of paper and draw a line in the middle. On one side write "DNR" and on the other side write "Resuscitate". As you go throughout your day, categorize each situation in your live under the perspective columns. At the end of the day, look at the list and be honest if each situation is listed under the correct categories.

Say this prayer - Father, there are many areas in my life where I have put up a DNR sign. Whether if it be in a relationship or another situation in my life...I stubbornly have that status written on my heart. I ask You today to reveal anything and everything that I need to see to get beyond the DNR status. The longer I stay bound to that status I cannot walk in the ways that You have purposed for me to walk in. Where forgiveness is needed within myself or for someone else, speak to my heart. Where reconciliation is needed within my life, speak to my heart. Let my heart be filled with Your love. Allow me to always know why I live and breathe. Allow me to see others as You see them – made in Your image. Let me truly see and understand why these situations need to be resurrected within Your will and for Your purpose. I thank You and Praise You. In Jesus' name...Amen.

#WDTFIMT Reading/Meditation

❑ Romans 9
❑ Matthew 5:23-26

Where does this fit in your testimony?

Based on what you read, what is your main take away? And why?

What are you thankful for today? Why?

Who can you do something nice for today? And how?

Study Notes

Follow the Leader

I was 16 when I got my license to drive. My dad, a former NY taxi driver, partially taught me how to drive…So you can only imagine what my "Driving Genes" look like. Although he began to teach me how to drive, those lessons didn't last too long but his habits stuck with me. We got on each other's nerves and didn't have any patience for each other. Luckily, I was still able to learn how to drive with the help of a private instructor. It was easy to learn from this person, although he was a stranger. I was able to see things from a different perspective and follow his lead while learning the most important Do's and Don'ts of driving.

#WDTFIMT Moment

I was driving home today and of course, I ended up in the ill-reputed Atlanta traffic. Luckily I've learned how to get to a place using more than one route. As I began to make my way to my alternate route, my bladder decided that it needed to make a bathroom stop. I've been drinking a lot of water…so what else should I expect? In the back of my mind, I'm rolling eyes and thinking where should I go. I then get my aha moment…I thought about stopping at Starbucks. I trust the presentation of their bathrooms AND I figured while I was there I can get a Triple Venti Vanilla Latté with extra syrup and whip cream. (I know that sounds like a lot…but it tastes like tea to me since I drink it on a regular basis). Sadly…I was more excited about getting to the latté than getting to the bathroom the moment I thought of Starbucks.

Anywho, as I'm driving a lady to my left signals to move over in my direction. I had to make a decision as to either speed up to get to my destination quicker or to slow down and allow her to get in front of me. Although my bladder was dancing, I decided to slow down and let her move over in front of me…Praying that she knew what she was doing so I can get to my destination with no delay because I was on a dual mission. Then it hit me…Have you ever noticed that when you drive you are following the lead of the person in front of you, while the person behind you is following your lead??? We do this every day. We follow the lead of perfect strangers that drive. We drive trusting that the person would be mindful of how they handle/maneuver their car. We drive trusting that we would make it to our destination with no issues. If you think about it even further, we follow the lead of everyone that switches a lane and momentarily we have to make sure we adjust how we drive to get used to the new person that is in front of us. No different when we switch lanes, the person that is behind us has to temporarily adjust to our habits. If you have driven a car for years, then this is something that you can do in your sleep. BUT if someone makes the wrong move, makes the wrong turn, or makes a hard fast break...something is bound to happen and the aftermath would be nothing pretty.

Driving is no different than relationships and the things that we may deal with on an everyday basis. We have to be mindful of what we bring the table. We also have to be mindful that when we drive a car, we may be driving in the same direction of other people but we are not necessarily going to end up at the same destination. We may be driving in the same direction, but many of us are driving at different speeds. I don't think it's possible that everyone could ever drive at the same speed every time. Regardless, we are put in the position to follow someone else's lead as we make our way towards our final destination as leaders. But one question to ask yourself, as it was presented to me, how willing are you to humble yourself in order to follow the lead of someone else as you are leading others...Even if the person is a stranger. I thought about this in depth...yes in the short time as I made my way to bathroom freedom and the GREATEST latté ever.

Work – Regardless of where you work and regardless of the title you hold, you have to follow the lead of someone. Ironically, we do not see God the same way we see the CEO of a major corporation, but we still have to follow the rules of the CEO. We are trusted as leaders in some form of fashion to carry out the mission and vision of the company as a whole. Do you follow the leader easily at work as you should or do you make it hard for others to follow you? What if you owned your own business? Wouldn't you want your employees to trust you and follow your lead as you trust them to lead as well?

Ministry – Like the workplace, you have to deal with a multitude of personalities. Regardless of the schizophrenic episodes that you may experience within a given ministry, do you ever catch the schizophrenic bug and speak against the leadership of the church after hearing a great message? Or do you make it a point to follow the vision that God gave to the pastor/leader of the church? We all claim to be Christians, but when it comes to certain things in the church we are quick to shout "Amen" to all of the things that we condemn others for...but we justify why we act the way we do when we are put on the spot for the lack of leadership skills/qualities that may be exhibited at a particular moment.

Marriage – This is one area that I feel two people should ALWAYS drive in the same car...REGARDLESS of the direction they are going. May seem impossible, but it actually is possible. We all have different callings/purposes, but when dealing with a marriage they mesh into one somehow – if done the right way. Women are still considered leaders within a purpose, but in a marriage, women should not hijack the car keys at all times and declare themselves the driver. (Yes...I am fully aware of me not potentially making any new friends after making a statement as such. BUT ask me if I care?). Women should see it as a privilege to be a passenger in the marriage car but also see the importance of taking over the steering wheel when the men need assistance in doing so. And that means to take over the steering wheel still seeing the marriage as a ministry/partnership...Not a hostile takeover. Some men may be stubborn at times of asking for directions, but in order for those men to learn how to lead they have to circle I-285 a few times in order for them to see that they have to be a good leader - eventually asking for directions. AND just because men are to be the primary drivers, majority of the time, does not mean for them to drive recklessly - eventually putting everyone's life in jeopardy.

Friendships – You will always be in the presence of people that you tend to act like. From the way you talk to the way you dress...But are you truly cultivating friendships where your life still remains within purpose? Are you leading everyone or are they following you? Either way, you look at who's following who...if the direction leads towards a dead end things will eventually collide.

God – As I thought of all of this, something else hit me. Following God's lead is like driving a car with NO hands. Your foot is on the gas pedal, but you cannot control the wheel. You can't control the turns you are to make. You can't control the speed you drive in. You can't even control when and where you have to pump the breaks. You do have a choice in a lot of things...BUT to follow God's lead is allowing Him to drive the car even if you are in the driver's seat. You truly have to want to follow God's lead and not have control of the car at all. Struggling with God will eventually cause your car to spin out and cause a wreck.

I'm sure that you can put yourself in more than one of the categories that are explained above. I don't know what direction you are going in. I don't know what turns you are going to make. You may be at a complete stop and in a traffic fiasco, but you have to remember that regardless of the situation you are leading someone as you are following someone else's lead. You also have to remember that as you lead others, God should always remain in control. You determine the ease of your journey. Even if you end up driving through a storm and the windshield is foggy, God can still guide you through allowing others to be able to see your break lights so you can still effectively lead them in the direction that you are traveling in. Ignoring the rules of driving can eventually make you total your car.

#WDTFIYOURT Challenge

How would you rate yourself as a leader within the Kingdom? If others were to give you a report card about yourself (i.e. Your Love Walk, How you deal with others, etc.), what would people say? What do you need to do to get things right? Think about the answers and write what comes to your heart in your journal.

#WDTFIMT Reading/Meditation

- ❑ Judges 5
- ❑ Proverbs 12

Where does this fit in your testimony?

Based on what you read, what is your main take away? And why?

What are you thankful for today? Why?

Who can you do something nice for today? And how?

Study Notes

Urban Billy Madison

Parenting does not come with a complete manual. I only say that because the Bible does mention how a child should be raised…And even in that, I think God was being humorous in His own way on what that was. I think, as a parent, you have to be creative on how you raise your child and even discipline them, but still according to the word of God. Only because, not all children are the same. Not only that…You just have to find a way to stay "sane" so to speak when your child does something that would make you pull your hair out.

#WDTFIMT Moment

For those who know me automatically knows how I feel about my children's education, along with how my children should approach their education. For those who know me would also know that I expect a lot of today's educators as well. I have no problem saying what I have to say if a teacher is not working at his/her full potential (regardless if my child is their student or not), nor do I have a problem doing the same with my children.

I am privileged to say that my kids are GREAT kids. I have to sometimes remember that my DNA is a part of them, so when they say something or do something…I just have to breathe and maybe repent for things that I may have done or said as a child. They both have my mouth. They both have my facial expressions. They've inherited ALOT from me, so you can only imagine what my everyday life is like with the two of them. Most people love to come to the house because it is non-stop comedy central for them. I would say one thing my son may not have inherited from me is to know how to do something he's really not supposed to do while not getting caught. My daughter, on the other hand, she will do something she is not supposed to do and would very rarely get caught… Something that I pray about…only because I knew how I was at her age (That's a WHOLE different #WDTFIMT Moment.) BUT if she does get caught 9 times out of 10 she will just say "Yeah, I did it."

My son's fourth-grade year was a VERY interesting school year. I think within that one year I may have gone off on his teacher, the principal, and him a few times that I can't count. My tolerance for pettiness, laziness, and excuses is VERY low. (Something I'm working on…Honestly, I am. But all three of them exhibited all qualities throughout that year.) One day I got a call from the 4th Grade Counselor to let me know that my son was supposed to be taking a test, but was drawing instead. Keep in mind this was a test that was required by the state…Nonetheless, even if it was not a state-mandated test, he shouldn't have been conducting his own art class. Everyone at his school knew that if I received a phone call about anything, I would eventually show up at the school...They just didn't know when.

I decided to go to the school early that next morning. I did not make any appointments. Nor did I call ahead of time. I just showed up. The principal and counselor knew that if I was in the building they would eventually have to see me face to face...Which did happen the moment I walked in. My son was there, as well, so I could only imagine what he was thinking. Here is what took place:

Principal and Counselor: Good Morning

Me: Morning. Not going to make this long, because I need to go. Apparently, my son feels he should doodle on paper while he is supposed to take a test so we are going to fix that right now. Effective IMMEDIATELY, I am withdrawing him from the 4th grade and demoting him back to Kindergarten. He is NOT to be removed from Kindergarten until I say so and until either one of you feel he has learned a lesson. And if is up to me...He'll stay there for the rest of the year.

Quiet
Crickets
Pins dropping can be heard

Principal and Counselor: Are you serious?

Me: Yes. He will be at school tomorrow with nothing but a nap mat, lunch, and crayons. He is to do the work the kindergarten students are working on. And NO he cannot act as if he is big brother...Helping out the students as if he knows it all. He is to be treated EXACTLY like a kindergarten student since that is how he wants to act.

Principal and Counselor: OK

Me: Great. I will touch base with you soon. Any issues...You know where to find me.

You may be questioning did I really do this. Yes. My kids know that I don't have it all in the head when it comes to creatively disciplining them, but they try their luck anyway. The school faculty always knew how I am, but whatever was put in place was worth the overall outcome. My son actually cried the 1st day he had to re-attend Kindergarten. He was humble all of the days that he was in his new class. His friends knew what happened the moment it happened. It was the latest news going around in school. Ask me if I cared. Nope. Even being the PTA President, at that time, I didn't care. I didn't care about the title that I held…I was a parent first. Eventually, my son was promoted back to the 4th grade knowing that if I was to get a phone call again, I would make the teacher hold him back the next school year. You also have to keep in mind, my son missed days of 4th-grade work so when he got back to class he had to do double work to catch up.

This incident happened a year ago, which is when #WDTFIMT was birthed. When I looked at what was going on in my life, at that time and even now, this event stuck out. Have you ever noticed how we are held back in life or demoted spiritually when we do something wrong or do not pass the tests that we are given. We sometimes even have the audacity to shake our fists at God in frustration of us being held back, but do we really understand why He is holding us back? Here is a list of why:

- Being immature
- Not being ready for promotion
- Acting out of disobedience
- Not listening
- Being impatient
- Deviating away from God's Plan

The list can go on, but does any of this make sense?? We cannot move forward until we are doing exactly what we have been told to do and how we were instructed to do it. We are so quick to boast about who we are and that we are Christians, but are we truly doing what we are supposed to be doing? Believe me, I've come up with some bright ideas and plans of my own, but I can say one thing in me doing so…It got me nowhere. It didn't matter who I boasted to be or what I was capable of doing. I was stuck in a particular place in life and some things were even set back because of me doing what I wanted to do. I may have seen some "movement" in areas of my life, but it was not the permanent moves that I should've made.

I don't know where you are in this particular moment of your life, but I'm sure some of you are stuck on "Do Not Pass Go" only because you may have done something that you weren't supposed to do or you just have not listened at all. God speaks and when He does you better listen. Just as a parent would tell their child to do something, God does too…Leaving NO room for negotiations or anything else. Just as a parent expects their child to act and conduct themselves a certain way, God expects the same from us. We cannot keep playing god in our own lives and still expect for the true God, Himself, to bless us and expand our territory spiritually. If we keep doing it our way, we are only setting ourselves up for setbacks and demotions.

#WDTFIYOURT Challenge

Answer this...What has God told you to do and you haven't done it? Write down every answer that comes to mind and make it a point to reflect on those items until it reaches your spirit. Ask God to take the lead as you follow His instructions.

Say this prayer - Father in all things that I am to do, let me be obedient and diligent. I know at times I may go against Your plan/word and setbacks are put in place, but from this day forward I can do nothing but follow the plan that You have set in place. I also know that with You in my corner I can pass all tests that are presented to me. Let me be an example to those around me. Let me not waiver when the tests do come. I at least know that You already know the outcome of the test. So let me be reminded that as I go through those tests, You have already worked everything out for Your glory. None of this is about me. It is about You and Your purpose in my life. Let me be reminded that the purpose You have declared over my life is not for me, but it is to be the benefit of those that cross my path. I thank You and I praise You. In Jesus' name...Amen.

#WDTFIMT Reading/Meditation

- ❑ Exodus 14
- ❑ Numbers 14

Where does this fit in your testimony?

_____

_____

_____

_____

_____

_____

Based on what you read, what is your main take away? And why?

_____

_____

_____

_____

_____

_____

What are you thankful for today? Why?

_____

_____

_____

Who can you do something nice for today? And how?

_____

_____

_____

_____

_____

_____

Study Notes

Split Second Sacrifice

Have you ever wondered how long it took for someone to realize that a car needed breaks in order to stop the car properly and safely? The car, itself, is a genius idea…But the cars that we drive today are not the same cars that were designed in the past.

#WDTFIMT Moment

Yesterday was a VERY long day. It seemed routine…Until that very split second.

5:00 a.m. – Wake up. Struggle to get out of bed.

5:05 a.m. – Thank God for waking me up. Ask for divine knowledge to walk in purpose.

5:15 a.m. – Think about the things that matter most. Think about the desires of my heart.

6:00 a.m. – Devotion. Get ready for work. Think about the next best thing for some clients.

8:00 a.m. – Drop the kids off before heading to the office.

9:00 a.m. to I Lost Track of Time – Meetings. Calls. Lots of e-mails. Pray that God will get me through. More meetings. More calls. More e-mails.

Trying to Figure Out What Time It Is – Thank God for the small things. Pick up kids. Walk dogs. Go to the store.

Somewhere Around 9:45 p.m. – Split second sacrifice and didn't think twice…

It was either me or my son. It was raining and I was driving as safe as I knew how to…But obviously, someone else was not thinking the same way. As I left the local grocery store, I proceeded to drive since I had the right-of-way. At the corner of my eye and in the canal of my ears…I see and hear a car halting on its breaks so hard that there was nothing left for me to do but to break at the same time so I would get hit before my son did. We all know water and rubber do not mix, so there was a gamble as to whether or not my car would stop with the other car directly adjacent to me or in the spine of my son. Something one would never think about having to decide throughout the day, but it was a decision that had to be made.

An experience as such isn't worth the "Mother of the Year Award." An experience as such is just a reminder that I am a mother before anything in life. And if it cost me my life…It's for a good reason. Regardless of how I feel. Regardless of what I think. It's a choice…But if I don't do it then who will? After catching my breath so I can continue to drive, I could only thank God as quick as I could. I felt as if I didn't thank Him fast enough though. I guess because I had to stop and look back to really see if my son and my car were still in one piece. I also had to lighten the experience and strike up a conversation to divert the attention elsewhere.

As I drove home, I could only think about how God made a decision in a split second when He knew that Jesus would become man to save us all. I don't think God had to think of whether or not He would have to weigh the options to make a decision as such. He just made the decision. God knew what needed to be done. Imagine if He was an indecisive God and dragged His feet on sacrificing His only Son. Imagine what our lives would be like. Imagine what this world would be like. All we could ever do is imagine, but because Jesus died for our sins we truly don't have to imagine anything. We can live our lives knowing that we are children of God and we have an AWESOME purpose to walk in for the glory of God.

#WDTFIYOURT Challenge

Do you know Jesus?

Say this prayer - Father, I can only thank You for the split second decision that You made. Because of what You decided, I now have eternal life. I now can live free from my past, while living within Your peace and forgiveness. Let me forever think of the split second decision that You made – enough to share the Great News of Your Word so others can know of the decision You made…Not just for me but for them as well. In Jesus' name. Amen.

#WDTFIMT Reading/Meditation

❑ Mark 15

Where does this fit in your testimony?

_____

_____

_____

_____

_____

_____

Based on what you read, what is your main take away? And why?

_____

_____

_____

_____

_____

_____

What are you thankful for today? Why?

_____

_____

_____

Who can you do something nice for today? And how?

_____

_____

_____

_____

_____

_____

_____

Study Notes

<u>GPS Signal Lost</u>

Technology, these days, still manages to blow my mind once in a while.   Every day my phone automatically pulls up a routine route at any given time of the day. It tells me the outlook on traffic, the average speed everyone else is traveling, etc. Do I have enough time to lollygag? Or do I need to leave ahead of time to drive an alternate route? It is as if my phone knows my schedule, my habits, and my every move. It is sometimes scary to know that technology has come this far, but it is also awesome to know that this is just the beginning. I still feel gypped some kind of a way though. After all of the years that I watched the *Jetsons*, I grew up believing that I would be able to drive a flying car and walk through a tunnel to get dressed in no time by the year 2000.

#WDTFIMT Moment

Driving to an unfamiliar place.

Turn Left in 2.5 Miles

Turn Right on

Long Pause

GPS Signal Lost

At the very moment I heard "GPS Signal Lost," I was actually able to feel as disappointed as Beth (that is what I call the GPS announcer) did. It's as if Beth seemed lost, herself, and had to regain her thoughts while waiting on something to give her the next move. Something else I can relate to…

These past few weeks I have come to a place in life where I can only say "I don't know" about a lot of things. If it has nothing to do with business, contributing to someone's purpose or the kids…I really don't want to be bothered. I don't communicate with a lot of people…Not in a snobbish way, but in a way where I truly don't feel like answering the simplest question like "How are you?" Not many know how to deal with an answer of "I don't know." It then becomes a moment of 10,000 questions…and they all get the same answer. Guess what that answer is. If you thought "I don't know"…You got it!

To me, it's about taking care of what matters, at the moment, and everything else is optional. Those that I talk to on an everyday basis is tied to what matters in some kind of way. If they weren't…then I really wouldn't have much to say. Some would say that I'm worn out. Some would say that I need a break. I don't think that's the case. I can honestly say that my patience for people that aren't ready to move forward in life…is none existent. I can honestly say that there are some situations in my life that I am about to put on the back burner or have done so already – only because some situations, in particular, are becoming irrelevant…At least I feel they are.

It's been a time of silence, within myself…And a time of silence from God. I think about Joyce Meyer's sermon "The Silent Years"…something that I may have to go back to. She said, within the sermon, that being in a time of silence isn't a bad thing, but you have to bring yourself to a place of remembering the things that God has promised. That's where the tournament of tug-of-war comes into play. I think because of where I'm at this moment in life, it's not a focus of keeping score or even trying to win…It's a moment of thinking of the things that I think I heard God promised compared to what I know He promised. There are a lot of things that don't make sense. Then again…is anything supposed to make sense when God is bigger than all of the human population combined?

I can list all areas of my life where there is a promise or the thought of a promise, but ultimately I have to go back to the original message of "The Silent Years" and see where I need to readjust my thinking and anything else for that matter. I don't know who is stuck in the same place that I am, but I know I have been prompted to write this for a reason. Does it make sense to me fully? Nope. But again when is anything supposed to make sense when God knows what He is doing? I can only follow the prompt and encourage you to view the same message that I saw. Hopefully, the message will touch your spirit in some kind of way.

#WDTFIYOURT Challenge

Search for the video below and write down how you can relate to the message that is given.

Joyce Meyer
"The Silent Years"

#WDTFIMT Reading/Meditation

- ❑ Psalm 28
- ❑ Matthew 26:57-68

Where does this fit in your testimony?

_____

_____

_____

_____

_____

_____

Based on what you read, what is your main take away? And why?

_____

_____

_____

_____

_____

What are you thankful for today? Why?

_____

_____

_____

_____

Who can you do something nice for today? And how?

_____

_____

_____

_____

_____

_____

Study Notes

<u>Reminders That Speak Louder Than Words</u>

Isn't it amazing how the mind is designed to remember the smallest things that are easy to forget? Isn't even more amazing how God uses anything and everything to remind us of Him even when we least expect it.

#WDTFIMT Moment

As I got ready this morning, this reminder came to mind…

To live in God's permissive will means you are too selfish to live in His divine will. God has given us free will, but there comes a point in time where we must choose the right to exercise free will or to deny self altogether - ultimately allowing God to have complete control. It was not God's permissive will that Jesus died for our sins. NOR is it God's permissive will that He woke you up this morning.

These past few weeks have been…There isn't a word that comes to mind at the moment. I've been thinking about my purpose. I've been pouring into others. I've been praying about my innermost desires. I've been talking to God and He's been communicating back…Just not in ways that I've expected it.

Months ago I was told to put together a #WDTFIMT Girls' Day Out. I did exactly what I was told to do. I did the flyer. I did the e-mail blast. I even started to tell people, around me, about it. After a while, as things began to shift in my life, I just put the #WDTFIMT Girls' Day Out on the back burner. I thought to myself that I wasn't ready for something like this. I thought to myself that the task is bigger than myself and I can't accomplish it. I thought a lot of things…But what I thought ultimately didn't matter because God still had final say so as to how things go. I've been getting RSVP e-mails from people that I do not know. I've been wondering how they found out about the #WDTFIMT Girls' Day Out, but when it's all said and done it doesn't matter how they found out about it. Every time an RSVP e-mail comes in, it's a reminder of what my purpose is. It's also a reminder that my purpose is tied to others – whether if I know them or not.

Someone sent me an e-mail, earlier today, asking me if I was still writing my inspirational messages. She stated that she thought of me the other day because she missed the words that usually spanned her e-mail account. I responded to the e-mail and just stated that I haven't given up, but I was also in a place of being "quiet". I was caught off guard by this e-mail only because I never put much thought into how many people would really read what I send. Not only that, I get this e-mail after I've spent the past few days pouring into people around me. Am I always anxious to do this? I have to be honest and say no. I get nervous sometimes. I question what to say. I question how it will be received. I sometimes question a lot. The e-mail that I received was only a reminder that my words aren't taken lightly and some actually look to those words to help them get through any situation that they are currently facing.

In talking to God about my desires, I have to be reminded that my life belongs to Him. I want more kids. I want to be able to share my life and ministry with someone who is as unique as I am, while I support his purpose as well. I want a lot of things…But the one thing that I have to remember is that I need to have all that God intends for me to have in His divine will. I've learned over the years that being in God's permissive will is equivalent to having imitation meat with government cheese…It's not the real thing and will never equate to it. I think while I was getting ready for the day, I had to be reminded that God's will for my life cannot be duplicated, manipulated, nor imitated.

The title of this devotion can be deemed as an ironic oxymoron in some kind of way. You may have asked yourself, "How can a reminder speak louder than words?" The satire of all of this is that every reminder that was given to me was communicated with words in some kind of way. BUT when you know the reminders are from God, they are not to be taken lightly and are spiritually louder than the words that you may have read/heard. I have a choice of ignoring these reminders. I have a choice of operating in God's permissive will. I have a choice in a lot of things, but as each day goes by my need and want for God is more than my need for breath itself.

#WDTFIYOURT Challenge

I don't know how many of you are reading this, let alone can relate to this…But I'm sure God has been reminding you of something, in ways that you least expect Him to. I challenge you to really take heed of the reminders that He is giving you and walk within His divine will. The moment you make the choice to do so, your existence will take on a new meaning that you would never forget.

#WDTFIMT Reading/Meditation

- ❑ John 6:38-40
- ❑ Hebrews 13:20-21

Where does this fit in your testimony?

_____
_____
_____
_____
_____
_____

Based on what you read, what is your main take away? And why?

_____
_____
_____
_____
_____

What are you thankful for today? Why?

_____
_____
_____

Who can you do something nice for today? And how?

_____
_____
_____
_____
_____
_____

Study Notes

Is God Your Home Depot?

For some reason, Home Depot has become my new found place to be at least once a week. I go there for the little things (i.e. Light Bulbs, Mops, etc.). To be quite honest, I knew the store existed but I never saw a need to go there. I've always settled for the convenience of Wal-Mart being my one stop shop kind of place. Home Depot is a store that excites you and overwhelms you at the same time. It has wood down one aisle and bathroom fixtures down another. You can buy all of the materials you need to build an entire compound if you wanted to. As long as you have the plans in place to accomplish a task, Home Depot has every supply that you would need.

#WDTFIMT Moment

Every time I walk into Home Depot I'm amazed. There is so much you can do when it comes to Do-It-Yourself (DIY) projects. There is an aisle of DIY manuals. They even have mini workshops that allow you to put your DIY skills to practice before accomplishing the final task. The closest that I've come to DIY's projects consisted of me putting together a T.V. stand, 2 desks, and a bookcase. I've done all 4 in a time span of 5 years...so that shows you where my handy dandy interests lie.

As I walked down the aisles last week, I was geeked to know that if I ever came up with a DIY project idea I can rely on Home Depot to assist with the project. I began to look at it from a spiritual standpoint, the more I walked down the cleaning supply aisle. Have you ever thought about how God gives you ideas and revelations, but you sometimes wonder how in the world you will accomplish what He's given you? Then it hit me...God is Home Depot when it comes to ANYTHING and EVERYTHING in life. He's already written the manual for any and every "project" so you know what to expect while walking in purpose, how to counteract seen and unforeseen situations, etc. (the Bible). He always provides the materials you need to complete the project (spiritually, mentally, physically, and financially). God even provides the blueprint on how each "project" is to be implemented detail to detail - plans that are given to us in visions and revelations. We attend the DIY workshops (Life) more than we know it. The more I thought about this, the more I began to question if I have truly relied on God to be Home Depot in my life.

There comes a point in life where you can no longer use the excuse of self-getting in the way of God's plans – especially when you are a child of God and you know the words He's already spoken to you. God has given us all that we need to walk in purpose, but we allow self to be boasted or pitied in the process – so much that we tend to forget who is to be glorified in anything that we experience or accomplish in life. God has always intended for us to need Him. I'd take it a step further to say that it is intended for us to want Him…not just need Him. I initially went to Home Depot because I needed to buy something, but because I've seen all that Home Depot can offer my needs have now turned into wants. It's no different when it comes to God. I no longer need to know the details or outcome of a plan upfront. I want whatever plans that God has purposed for me. I no longer need the materials that (I think) are required to carry out the plans. I want what God has for me because He already knows the outcome of the plans that He set before me. I no longer try to schedule or orchestrate what "life workshops" I want to attend. I want to accept every invitation that is offered to me because the DIY projects have now become GADINLI (God Already Did It…Now Live It!) projects. Does any of this make sense? I hope it does.

#WDTFIYOURT Challenge

I challenge you this week to get inspired to experience any and every GADINLI Project that is destined to take place in your life. Go to your nearest Home Depot or supply store and just walk down the aisles. Imagine that store being a place that holds anything/everything that God has for you in purpose/life. Think of each wrench and screwdriver as being a tool that God has already given you to carry out a plan. Think of all of the supplies as the supplies that have been granted by God specifically for your purpose. Think about all that God has given you in visions and revelation. Once you've thought about all of that, think of how God already knows the outcome of what He's given. At the very second, you have your Ah-Ha Moment, walk out of the store and live out what God has put before you.

#WDTFIMT Reading/Meditation

- ❑ Philippians 4:19
- ❑ Jeremiah 29:11

Where does this fit in your testimony?

_____

_____

_____

_____

_____

_____

Based on what you read, what is your main take away? And why?

_____

_____

_____

_____

_____

What are you thankful for today? Why?

_____

_____

_____

Who can you do something nice for today? And how?

_____

_____

_____

_____

_____

_____

Study Notes

In Blank Amount of Years

The majority of people, living in today's society, have set some kind of goal that they may have written in their journal or scribbled on a napkin after a near death experience.

"In 10 years I'll quit my job

"In 8 years I'll have enough money to retire"

"In this amount of time I can do this and in that amount of time I can do that."

The goal possibilities go on and on. In setting goals, people sometimes become fixated with reaching those goals. And sometimes those goals statements turn into "If only…" statements.

"If only I had more money, my problems would go away."

"If only if I was more advanced in my career, I'd be farther along in life."

"If only I would be doing this or that by now given my age."

"If only so and so would make situations easier in my life…"

Have you ever thought of how the "If only…" statements make you feel even worse that you haven't achieved your goal or have what you want in life? Better yet, have you ever stopped to think why you haven't fully reached that goal that you've set for yourself or why you don't have what you want in life?

#WDTFIMT Moment

These past 2 months have literally seemed like a warp to me. Something happened that I never expected to happen. Something happened and it is trying every ounce of faith in me. People know that when I get "challenged" in life, I will bury myself in things that need to get taken care of and somewhere along being buried I quiet myself to hear the things that I need to hear. Whatever happened had nothing to do with goals or any "If only…" moments (At least I think so), but it does have something to do with matters of the heart…real close to heart. In all of my quiet time, I have been guided in things that would push my faith beyond any goal that I may have ever set in my life. In all of this, I have been pushed even more to depend on a God that I say is awesome and can never fail me. In all of this, I have been pushed to even hope for the best even through moments of me wanting to throw my hands up and say "Forget This!" because of the way things may look at the current moment. In all of this, I have been put in a position to look at my Source for anything and everything. So what does this have anything to do with how I started this message... Believe me, there is a point to all of this.

Although what happened has nothing to do with goals, I have been able to listen to the things that others may be dealing with to speak on... Somewhere in all of that, I get the revelations that I need to hear for myself as well. God has promised A LOT of things in His word. He is so set on His promises that He even showed me this point... The moment anyone is born, God has to fulfill His promises within that person's life as long as they do what they need to do pertaining to Him. How awesome is that to even know? If God is obligated to fulfill those promises within your life just for you being born (and you doing what you need to do)... Then why be so fixated on a goal (source) that may not be a full part of your divine purpose?

I think that's where a lot of us miss it. We get so bogged down with the things that we have not accomplished or the lack of things... But have you ever questioned were you even supposed to accomplish that one thing within God's will? Or have you become so fixated on the "source" that you've forgotten the one true Source that reigns in your life. God may want you to accomplish something in half the time of your set goal because He has something bigger and better for you to accomplish, but because you didn't consult Him on what you need to do your goal will always be something that you can't fully reach in peace/fulfillment. Something will always seem missing or never enough. You will always feel as if you're running on a hamster wheel - getting nowhere within your goal. You then start being even harder on yourself and then start with your "If only..." statements. For every "If only..." statement you make, you are pushing yourself away from a moment of tapping into your Source that already has the solution to anything that you may be dealing with.

In everything that we deal with, we have to learn how to let go of any controlling habits that we may have in life – even when it comes to our personal goals/desires in life. We have to let go of what we want and consult God on what He knows we need to do or have in our lives. I'm not saying that God can't give you the desires of your heart.... But wouldn't the process be so much easier if you consult God on the things that you desire before setting on a path that leads to nowhere? Life's situations will always try to throw us off course, but if we consult God on the will He has for our lives we can build up a strength/faith that is impermeable. As life's situations come up, beyond your control, just turn them over to God and don't take them back. The more we take things back, the more we will be stuck in a place of not moving forward within our purpose. The more we take things back, the harder it would be for

God to show us the things we need to see in order to be great within His purpose.

We have to keep in mind that the things we go through may not just be about ourselves, but may also about how we would impact someone's purpose that is a part of our life. There may be a lesson for someone else to learn as God deals with their heart for the things that they may be doing, along with preparing us for the bigger picture. If you truly believe that God has put someone or something in your life for a purpose, you have to hold fast to His promises even if things feel as if they are being snatched from you in every direction. Keep in mind that He knew everything and anything that you would face in life before you were even born. So now that you are alive, live within His promises while reaching His goals and everything else will work out far greater than you can ever imagine.

#WDTFIYOURT Challenge

Stop putting limits on God! Make a list of everything that you've put time limits on and feel that God has to comply with your timeframe. Once you've completed that list, say "I let go of (List Item) and I give it to God completely – not taking it back!" Say it until it reaches the depths of your spirit. If you have to write it, shout it, sing it…Whatever! Make the proclamation and release anything/everything the God. Take the next few days to be in a quiet space within God to truly hear what you need to hear.

#WDTFIMT Reading/Meditation

- ❑ 1 Peter 2
- ❑ 2 Peter 3

Where does this fit in your testimony?

_____

_____

_____

_____

_____

Based on what you read, what is your main take away? And why?

_____

_____

_____

_____

_____

What are you thankful for today? Why?

_____

_____

_____

Who can you do something nice for today? And how?

_____

_____

_____

_____

_____

_____

_____

Study Notes

Do Not Hit Ignore!

Amazing how technology has changed over the years. From communication to coffee makers, there are a lot of things to brag about if you're one to have the latest cell phone or the best tasting coffee. Even though we've progressed over the years, I still feel duped for watching so many episodes of the Jetsons (That's a whole different story.)

#WDTFIMT Moment

I was reading the Bible this morning and what I read made me think (as it should). Somehow as I thought about what I read, I also began to think about how technology today has made it easy for us to do certain things...Like ignore people. If you own a cell phone then you know what I'm talking about. Nowadays, we can look at the phone and it will tell us who is calling by displaying the info on the screen. Some phones can even speak the person's name that is calling. How cool is that? If you're a gadget person like me, you'd have both options.

Remember back in the days when we only had one house phone that didn't have call waiting, caller ID, nor 3 way? It was hard to ignore a phone call because back then you didn't know who was calling and you just answered the phone in case it was important. Not today. Today we have it all and the IGNORE button on our phone is used quite often. There are very few reasons why I would ignore a call, but some people may have more than 1,000 which may only still boil down to 2 main reasons.

How many times within one day do you hit the IGNORE button when someone calls you? As I continued to read the Bible, I began to think about how many times in a day do we hit the IGNORE button when God is calling (speaking to) us. Unlike the people that call us, God can still see us and hear us whenever we hit the IGNORE button. He sees our facial expressions. Hears us sucking our teeth. He sees the condition of our heart. He hears our thoughts...Amongst everything else that we may do when we don't want to be bothered by God. We can't come up with any excuses as to why we did hit the IGNORE button. We can try if we want to, but this is God we are talking about here. There are things that He will talk to us about and we automatically hit IGNORE - not thinking twice about it. There are things that He asks or tells us to do and we hit IGNORE. There is a long list of things that we can hit IGNORE on, but how would we really benefit anything from that?

I think we depend on self and live in our own free will so much that we eventually act as if God doesn't exist until something drastic happens and we end up calling on Him. What if God hit His IGNORE button when you called out to Him? What if He stuck His fingers in His ears and sung a song at the top of His lungs to tune you out - as if He was a little child? That is sometimes how we act. Thankfully, God is AWESOME....BUT that does not give us the right to IGNORE Him or the purpose that He has spoken over our lives.

#WDTFIYOURT Challenge

For the rest of the year, count how many times you hit the IGNORE button when it comes to God. If you are counting, then you'd at least know how many times you've missed your blessings, denied your purpose, and everything else. You'd also be aware of how many times God could've hit the IGNORE button when it comes to you. Just the thought of God ignoring me is scary enough. Hopefully, it would have some effect on you.

#WDTFIMT Reading/Meditation

- ❏ Proverbs 10
- ❏ Romans 10

Where does this fit in your testimony?

_____

_____

_____

_____

_____

Based on what you read, what is your main take away? And why?

_____

_____

_____

_____

_____

_____

What are you thankful for today? Why?

_____

_____

_____

_____

Who can you do something nice for today? And how?

_____

_____

_____

_____

_____

_____

_____

Study Notes

<u>My Waiting Behavior</u>

If the word "patient" was in a picture dictionary, a picture of my face would not represent that word. Seriously...If you were to look up the word, this is what you will find:

pa·tient [pey-shuhnt]

noun
1. a person who is under medical care or treatment.
2. a person or thing that undergoes some action.
3. a sufferer or victim.

adjective
4.bearing provocation, annoyance, misfortune, delay, hardship, pain, etc., wit h fortitude and calm and without complaint, anger, or the like.
5. characterized by or expressing such a quality: a patient smile.

#WDTFIMT Moment

I have been going to the same nail salon for almost 8 years now. There are some things that I can accept substitutes for, but when it comes to my nails, feet, and eyebrows I will not compromise. When I walk through the door, everyone knows what I want and how I want...NO questions asked. Everyone knows how short my nails need to be cut, the colors I like for my toes, and the exact curve my eyebrows should be arched. How can I ever give that up?

I made an appointment one day to get my nails done. I forced myself to make the appointment because if I didn't I would've put off going to get my nails done. There is something about setting appointments that keeps me accountable. I figure if I set-up an appointment, the time has not only been set aside, but I am to respect the other person's time.

Anywho, I initially wanted to set-up an appointment with Mary (one of the owners of the nail salon). As I spoke to Mary, she stated that she was booked for the time that I needed, but her husband, Mike, was available. Don't get me wrong...I like Mike. This man is in his 70's and doesn't look a day over 40. He loves to chat, talk about what's going, etc. BUT he's a guy (No offense!). Of course, Mike takes pride in the work he does, but he doesn't put that oomph in my nails like Mary. Now Mike can do my toes...He is great with feet. He's never done my eyebrows before and I think we should keep it that way.

I arrived at my appointment 15 minutes early. As I walked in, everyone shouted "Hello" as they usually do. I glanced towards Mike's direction and someone was at his nail station. I thought to myself that he will be done in time for my appointment and I will be out in no time. Well, that didn't happen. I sat. I waited. I sat. I waited. I shifted. I sat. I waited some more. I did everything I could to stay up since it was a long day for me. I also had to catch myself when I felt myself becoming impatient. After 45 minutes, a daughter of Mike and Mary said that she could take care of my eyebrows. I sluggishly got into the chair and we began to chat. The process was completed in a little over 15 minutes, only because we were talking about my decision to homeschool the kids. After we got done talking, I was instructed to go to Mary's station. I didn't know if I was to walk, run, leap, or all of the above at the same time. You just do not know how that was music to my ears. Yes, it was almost an hour later from my initial appointment time…BUT I got what I initially wanted.

As I got my nails done, I began to think about what the outcome would've been if I got frustrated to a point of just leaving or having a negative attitude about the whole situation. I thought about how I would've lost out and not gotten what I initially wanted. But then as I thought about it further, I began to question "My Waiting Behavior" in other areas of my life. If I were to give myself a report card after doing some self-evaluations, I would more than likely have to repeat some lessons in order to bring my grades up. There are a lot of things, in life, that I know have been promised to me by God…BUT one thing that I always have to remember is that EVERYTHING happens in God's timing and not my own.

As I continued to get my nails done, I thought about what my life would've been like if I continued to live a life consumed of impatience. When you become impatient, you become a grouch, a meanie, and everything else that people DO NOT want to deal with. When you become impatient, you miss out on other opportunities that God has destined for you – in preparation for what is bigger and better to come. When you become impatient, you just miss out in life PERIOD. The word "patient" is a two-fold word. We are God's patients as we grow to become more patient in life. There comes a point, in your walk with God, when you have to get rid of all stopwatches, alarms, and everything else that reminds you time. If you don't, you will still be late getting to your appointed destination within purpose.

#WDTFIYOURT Challenge

It's funny that I am writing this…Then again it's not. I was TECHNICALLY supposed to write this over the weekend, but I was bound to my bed due to my back being non-functional. I received word today that one of my FAVORITE books is finally available on Kindle. I let someone borrow my original copy...And guess what happened?? The book is nowhere to be found.

The subject matter of the book ties right into this entry. Your challenge for the week is to purchase and read **In The Process Of Time: Victory Through Your Waiting Season**, by Andrea Diallo. Take your time to read this book. Believe it or not, I first read this book in 2010 and it has been a part of me since then. I know it will become a part of you in some way as well.

#WDTFIMT Reading/Meditation

- ❏ Isaiah 40
- ❏ Psalm 37

Where does this fit in your testimony?

Based on what you read, what is your main take away? And why?

What are you thankful for today? Why?

Who can you do something nice for today? And how?

Study Notes

No Pennies!!!

Toll booths may not be a favorite for most tax paying citizens that do not see a point in their existence. I'm one of those people. Some tolls are used by public authorities to generate revenue to repay a debt. Some tolls are collected to accumulate finances to build future road expansions and maintain roads, tunnels, bridges, etc. Some tolls are also used as general tax fund for local governments and may have little or nothing to do with transportation facilities.

#WDTFIMT Moment

One day I needed to get to a place that required me to get on the highway. Before I walked out of the house, I got an alert stating that there was a traffic jam in the direction that I was heading towards. I had to think of an alternate route because I wanted to arrive on time. The only route that was available and traffic free required me to pay a toll. Many people who know me would know that I do carry cash on me. So at this moment, I had to scramble for some change. I found a quarter. I found two dimes. I found ten pennies. I needed fifty cents to get through the toll and I knew I couldn't use pennies in the automatic toll. I looked in my drawers. I dumped everything out of my pocket book. I looked on the floor. I checked my tablet bag. Still nothing! I kept telling myself that I needed a nickel. Then something hit me and said, "You can use the pennies in the cashier lane and still get through the toll." DUH!!!! Why didn't I think of that to begin with? I've gone through the cashier lane plenty of times and paid with bills, and I didn't even think to use the pennies in the cashier lane.

As I thought of the solution that was revealed to me, I started to think about how many times I may have held myself back from passing through a "toll" only because my perception of my available resources were "unacceptable". Pennies were not acceptable in the automatic toll lane, but no one ever said that I still couldn't get through the toll. It's no different with what I am purposed to do. My resources may not add up to what I think I should have to fulfill my purpose, but in reality, I have everything that I need to move forward.

I have been on a journey within myself. I have also stepped back from a lot of things to re-evaluate where I am in life and where certain people fit in my life. I can honestly say that there are some people that I have put on the back burner because I felt that I have given my all to them and I just need to focus on self at the moment. This is something that I know that I need to do and however anyone fits into my big picture, they will take their rightful places back in my life slowly but surely. In all of this, I also have reminded myself that the resources that are before me fit somewhere in my purpose. Whether if it be a person, an opportunity, etc. it fits. I just need to know and see how it fits.

#WDTFIYOURT Challenge

I don't know where you are in life at this moment, but I'm sure you are in a place that many can relate to. You may be in a place of asking yourself how you can get to the next level within your purpose without the right resources. You may be wondering why you feel as if you are at a standstill, because you do not know which way you should go.

Take inventory of the things that you feel to be "unacceptable" resources to be used within your purpose. Once you have compiled a list, make it a point to look at those resources from a different point of view. Pray about how you are to really use those resources within your purpose and write down the revelations that you receive in your journal. From that point, ask God to make His plan impeccable within your spirit – allowing yourself to yield to His way and not yours.

#WDTFIMT Reading/Meditation

- ❑ 1 Kings 4
- ❑ 1 Kings 5

Where does this fit into your testimony?

Based on what you read, what is your main take away? And why?

What are you thankful for today? Why?

Who can you do something nice for today? And how?

Study Notes

A Spare Tire and Very Little Gas

I was driving one day, on my way to get gas, and one of the tires in the front went flat. I was frustrated. I had a car full of groceries. The kids were in the car. I was tried. It was already a long day and this was the last thing that I needed to deal with. I called my insurance company and they transferred me over to Roadside Assistance. They were able to GPS my location after I gave them permission to do so. After 25 minutes, a man pulled up, put the spare on and went about his business.

I pulled out from where I was originally located and drove less than half a block and made it to the gas station. I filled up the tank part of the way only because I was really tired and just wanted to get home. Waiting for the tank to fill up seemed like eternity. When I got in the car, there was only a quarter of a tank of gas in the car. Seriously? After spending as much as I did, I thought I would've had more in the tank. Anywho, I drove home, got the groceries out of the car, got the kids situated, got in my bed and I said whatever. I woke up the next day still tired and I really didn't care about much for a while.

#WDTFIMT Moment

For the past few weeks, I've been drained. I've been feeling as if I've been giving my all to my job, other people, and life overall – with very little to show for it…let alone extremely underappreciated. I've been feeling as if my direction towards my purpose has been discombobulated – slowly becoming non-existent. There have been days where I'm just so tired and want the day to be over with before I even get out of bed. I think I've said "I'm tired and done" so many times that I could come up with 8 remixed songs just using those words.

I got in the car one day and realized I was still driving with the same tank of gas that I original had when my tire went flat. I was thinking how that could be. Usually, a quarter of a tank would only last me a blink of an eye. I began to dismiss the whole thing altogether and then something hit me. Although I was driving with a spare tire and barely a quarter of a tank of gas, the present state of my car represented how my life is in God's hands. Just like my car, I've been functioning on a spare and very little gas – but surviving within the strength of God. If I was truly functioning on my own strength, I would just give up completely. During times as such, it is easy to continue to look at where things currently are rather than looking at how God wants you to see it. I'm not going to lie…There are some things that have come up and I honestly sought God (as if He disappeared), but ultimately He was right where He always have been – right there in the midst of whatever I was going through.

As I would always say, God gives me the strangest revelations at the most weirdest times – all for a good reason. This all came to me after something came up, within my life, hoping I could turn to someone that I honestly thought would understand and be able to handle me at my worse...But ultimately I turned to God and said I need to be rejuvenated. It was painful and relieving all at the same time. I guess painful in the sense that you would always want someone, you love, to be able to get you/truly support you even during a bad day and not take things "personal". I sometimes think that maybe it was bad timing within the whole situation altogether. I don't know. Someone actually told me that same week, that many people may not be able to handle me at my worse for MANY reasons, but mainly because my worse requires someone that is mature in faith and assurance in self. If anyone knows me I'm silly as can be...but also deep in a way that many can't handle let alone comprehend. If you add emotions to all of that, I can see why someone would have to be mature in faith and have an assurance in self. I'm not one to pacify anyone, so if you deal with me you have to have some kind of a backbone...If any of that makes sense.

#WDTFIYOURT Challenge

Take a moment and think about how things have been in your life and then begin to think about how your life would truly be like without God. Write down everything that comes to mind and then take a moment in between each thought and thank God for being who He is in your life. After that, look for those that may be going through the same thing that you've gone through and make it a point to share your testimony with them. If you don't find them right away, pray that God can use your testimony to help others in some kind of way.   Don't be surprised with the outcome of that prayer.

#WDTFIMT Reading/Meditation

- ❑ Psalm 6
- ❑ Job 29

Where does this fit in your testimony?

Based on what you read, what is your main take away? And why?

What are you thankful for today? Why?

Who can you do something nice for today? And how?

Study Notes

About the Author

EB is best described as a 21st Century Ambassador sent from heaven. A no-nonsense, verbal pugilist, guided and flowing by the Spirit of Almighty God. Purpose and destiny provide both the opportunities and parameters to her interaction with an individual. To some she is an author, to others, she is a life coach, to some she is just a name on the bottom of a blog or thought for the day, and to others, she is a dynamic force helping propel their dream into reality. EB's life's mission is simply to take each and every person God directs to her, and craft a unique plan, where her array of skills will assist in attaining the person's purpose and destiny

When you interact with Ebbie, "EB", Miss Blanca, or "her" you are assured that you will never be the same. "She" will challenge your assumptions, press you to introspection, make you question your core expectations, with laser precision cut to the heart of a matter, and walk away as if she did not start the bonfire that now consumes you! There is no mistaking her "works" in progress, nor is there any substitute in identifying the impression of those who have been touched by her. God has chosen her for such a time as this, to mold servant leaders for a new millennium.

EB is an author, an agent, a poet, a seer of the invisible realms of the heart, a mentor, a mother, a friend, a vessel of the Most High God, a public speaker, a spokesperson for a generation that has lost their voice, a champion of standards of excellence, a breath of fresh air in a world of moral staleness, and a walking contradiction between the reality of the realm of the Spirit and the "supposed" limitations of the mind.

She is simply EB.

Let's connect on social media!
@TheEBFactor I @MyUPath

To book EB for an event, please contact My U Path, Inc.
www.MyUPath.com I Info@MyUPath.com I 478.5MY.PATH

EB is available for the following:
- Speaking Engagements
- Event Hosting
- Discussion Panels

EB is affiliated with the following organizations:
- Kingdom Dominion Church – *Villa Rica, GA*
- The K.D.C. Authors Guild – *Villa Rica, GA*

www.ingramcontent.com/pod-product-compliance
Lightning Source LLC
LaVergne TN
LVHW061257060426
835508LV00015B/1400